Focus on Developmentally Appropriate Practice

Equitable & Joyful Learning with Infants and Toddlers

Marie L. Masterson & Ron Grady, EDITORS

Susan Friedman, SERIES EDITOR

National Association for the Education of Young Children

Washington, DC

National Association for the Education of Young Children

1401 H Street NW, Suite 600
Washington, DC 20005
202-232-8777 • 800-424-2460
NAEYC.org

NAEYC Books
**Senior Director, Publishing
& Content Development**
Susan Friedman

Director, Books
Dana Battaglia

Senior Editor
Holly Bohart

Editor II
Rossella Procopio

Senior Creative Design Manager
Charity Coleman

Senior Creative Design Specialist
Gillian Frank

**Publishing Business
Operations Manager**
Francine Markowitz

Through its publications program, the National Association for the Education of Young Children (NAEYC) provides a forum for discussion of major issues and ideas in the early childhood field, with the hope of provoking thought and promoting professional growth. The views expressed or implied in this book are not necessarily those of the Association.

The following chapters were previously published in the specified issues of *Young Children*: November 2015—Chapter 16; May 2017—Chapters 1 and 12; November 2017—Chapter 4; May 2020—Chapter 23; Spring 2021—Chapters 13, 17, and 20; Spring 2023—Chapter 9; Summer 2023—Chapters 8 and 14.

Text on page 35 is adapted from S. Erdman & L.J. Colker, with E.C. Winter, *Trauma and Young Children: Teaching Strategies to Support and Empower* (Washington, DC: NAEYC, 2020).

Chapter 25 is adapted from I.M. Escamilla, L.R. Kroll, D.R. Meier, & A. White, *Learning Stories and Teacher Inquiry Groups: Reimagining Teaching and Assessment in Early Childhood Education* (Washington, DC: NAEYC, 2021).

Chapter 11 is adapted from J. Luckenbill, A. Subramaniam, & J. Thompson, *This Is Play: Environments and Interactions that Engage Infants and Toddlers* (Washington, DC: NAEYC, 2019).

Chapter 21 is adapted from M.B. McMullen & D. Brody, *Infants and Toddlers at Play: Choosing the Right Stuff for Learning and Development* (Washington, DC: NAEYC, 2022).

Chapters 6, 7, and 22 are adapted from NAEYC, *Casebook: Developmentally Appropriate Practice in Early Childhood Programs Serving Children from Birth Through Age 8,* eds. P. Brillante, J.J Chen, S. Cuevas, C. Dundorf, E.B. Hoffman, D.R. Meier, G. Mindes, & L.R. Roy (Washington, DC: NAEYC, 2023).

Chapters 3 and 18 are adapted from NAEYC, *Developmentally Appropriate Practice in Early Childhood Programs Serving Children from Birth Through Age 8,* 4th ed. (Washington, DC: NAEYC, 2022).

The following selections were previously published on the NAEYC blog (NAEYC.org/resources/blog):

Chapter 15 is adapted from N. Abayan, "The Power of Pause: Moments of Silence and Early Emotional and Language Development," March 3, 2023.

Chapter 26 is adapted from N. Lazarte, "Dear Congress, It's Time to #SolveChildCare," July 13, 2022.

Permissions
NAEYC accepts requests for limited use of our copyrighted material. For permission to reprint, adapt, translate, or otherwise reuse and repurpose content from this publication, review our guidelines at NAEYC.org/resources/permissions.

Cover Photo Credits
Copyright © Getty Images: cover, xii, 9, 13, 19, 49, 73, 81, 104
Copyright © NAEYC: 58
Courtesy of the authors: 12, 16, 53, 54, 68, 105, 109, 110, 122

Library of Congress Control Number: 2023948195

ISBN: 978-1-952331-28-2

Item: 1170

Contents

About the Editors

Volume Editors

Marie L. Masterson, PhD, is the director of quality assessment at the McCormick Center for Early Childhood Leadership at National Louis University, where she oversees evaluation for ExceleRate Illinois. She holds a doctorate in early childhood education, is a licensed teacher, and is a national speaker and author of many books and articles that address research-based, practical skills for high-quality teaching, behavior guidance, quality improvement, and leadership. She is a contributing editor of *Developmentally Appropriate Practice in Early Childhood Programs Serving Children from Birth Through Age 8,* fourth edition, and coauthor of *Building on Whole Leadership: Energizing and Strengthening Your Early Childhood Program.* Dr. Masterson is a former higher education faculty teacher trainer and early childhood specialist for the Virginia Department of Education. She provides educational consulting and professional development training to child care programs, schools, and organizations engaged in quality improvement and equitable teaching initiatives.

Ron Grady, MSEd, engages in work centered on the social worlds and peer cultures of young children, wondering how lived experience is both constructed within and revealed throughout play, the creation of art and narrative, and visual media such as photography and film. He taught preschool at NOLA Nature School in New Orleans for many years. Ron is a doctoral student in education at the Harvard Graduate School of Education and holds a master's degree in early childhood education from the Erikson Institute. He is the author of *Honoring the Moment in Young Children's Lives: Observation, Documentation, and Reflection* (Redleaf Press) and many articles on early childhood topics. He is also the author and illustrator of the children's book *What Does Brown Mean to You?* Ron serves on the editorial boards of both the *Harvard Educational Review* and *Voices of Practitioners.*

Series Editor

Susan Friedman is senior director of publishing and content development at NAEYC. In this role, she leads the content development work of NAEYC's books and periodicals teams. Ms. Friedman is coeditor of *Each and Every Child: Teaching Preschool with an Equity Lens.* She has extensive prior experience creating content on play, developmentally appropriate uses of media, and other topics for educators and families. She has presented at numerous educational conferences, including NAEYC's Professional Learning Institute and Annual Conference, the South by Southwest Education (SXSW EDU) Conference & Festival, and the School Superintendents Association's Early Learning Cohort. She began her career as a preschool teacher at City and Country School in New York City. She holds degrees from Vassar College and the Harvard Graduate School of Education.

Focus on Developmentally Appropriate Practice
Equitable and Joyful Learning Book Series

In this series, each book presents essential, foundational information from both NAEYC's position statement on developmentally appropriate practice and the fourth edition of *Developmentally Appropriate Practice in Early Childhood Programs Serving Children from Birth Through Age 8*. The books provide early childhood educators with the context and tools for applying developmentally appropriate practice in their work with specific age groups: infants and toddlers, preschoolers, kindergartners, and children in the primary grades. The foundational content is supported by examples of developmentally appropriate practice in real classrooms, illustrated through articles from NAEYC's books and periodicals, *Young Children* and *Teaching Young Children,* and through new material.

Developmentally Appropriate Practice

An Introduction

What Is Developmentally Appropriate Practice?

Developmentally appropriate practice is about effective teaching and joyful, engaged learning. It is a framework that guides the thinking and work of early childhood educators to create healthy, respectful, and responsive learning environments in which children thrive. It requires both meeting children where they are—which means that teachers must get to know them well—and helping them reach goals that are both challenging and achievable. NAEYC defines developmentally appropriate practice as "methods that promote each child's optimal development and learning through a strengths-based, play-based approach to joyful, engaged learning" (NAEYC 2020, 5). But no single method is appropriate in all settings or with all children. Educators use several sources of information to make intentional decisions about what's developmentally appropriate for *this* child at *this* time. These sources include what is known from research about child development, each child's individual characteristics, and each child's and family's context. Applying developmentally appropriate practice, then, means gaining the tools to build on children's strengths and knowledge so you can set goals and provide experiences that are suited to their learning and development.

Besides being an approach to teaching, developmentally appropriate practice is a position statement. Developed in the mid-1980s, NAEYC's original position statement on developmentally appropriate practice was a response to inappropriate teaching practices and expectations for preschool and kindergarten children. The statement has since been expanded to include children from birth through age 8. It remains focused on supporting equitable, high quality learning experiences for all young children. The position statement emphasizes the need for teachers to have a foundational knowledge of child development and a wide set of skills to support children's learning. The position statement also calls for teachers to embrace children's cultural, linguistic, and racial and ethnic diversity as well as individual learning needs and development. Effective educators learn who their children and families are and recognize the unique, multiple assets each brings to the learning community.

The fourth edition of *Developmentally Appropriate Practice in Early Childhood Programs Serving Children from Birth Through Age 8* examines developmentally appropriate practice in more detail. That book expands on the important concepts of the position statement with contributions from early childhood experts and champions of high-quality early learning experiences. The book and position statement, along with the advancing equity position statement and the book *Advancing Equity and Embracing Diversity in Early Childhood Education: Elevating Voices and Actions*, present integrated resources for all early childhood educators, regardless of their role or the ages of the children they serve.

As an educator, use the position statement on developmentally appropriate practice and the accompanying resources to get an overview of the ideas and components of developmentally appropriate practice. Reflect on your current practice and develop goals to improve your practice so that you are responding to children's learning needs within the larger context of their culture, language, racial identity, and other social identities.

Using the Three Core Considerations to Make Teaching Decisions

Effective early childhood educators use three core considerations to make decisions about curriculum and teaching: commonality, individuality, and context.

Here we briefly outline each of these and provide some examples to help you connect the core considerations to your work.

Commonality

Research on how children learn and develop provides several principles of human development and learning that are true for all children (see "Principles of Child Development and Learning," below). Teachers need a clear understanding both of how children learn and develop and what teaching practices are effective. However, learning is also greatly influenced by culture, experience, and individual characteristics. Within general progressions, development will look different for each child. For example, play is a foundational way children learn, but it can look different based on a child's culture and experiences. While children of various social, cultural, and linguistic backgrounds develop similarly in many ways, their specific identities and the history around those identities help shape their development and learning. It is important to understand the common characteristics of children's development and learning and how they may take unique forms.

Individuality

Each child is a unique individual but also a member of family and community. Effective educators get to know each child and family. They see individual differences—including children's personalities, abilities, knowledge, interests, cultural and social identities, home languages, and approaches to learning—as assets to build on. For example, Francisco is a dual language learner who speaks Mixtec and Spanish. He is learning English as a third language. Knowing this about Francisco helps his teacher make decisions about how to effectively support his learning. Understanding each child and their individual characteristics will influence your planning, instruction, and assessment.

Context

To fully support each child's development and learning, teachers consider the children's and families' social and cultural contexts, as well as their own. As an educator, you might hold certain biases (whether known or unknown) based on your own upbringing, your personal experiences, and your identities. Be reflective about your

practices to ensure that you are not teaching and making decisions from a deficit perspective based on stereotypes and misinformation about certain groups. For example, when Adah arrives in your infant classroom, you learn that she is carried in a sling at home. Her family speaks Hindi and keeps a strict schedule for caring routines. You may wonder what play experiences Adah has had, whether she will adjust to your setting, and whether the family will be open to floor play and tummy time. Rather than make assumptions about the family's childrearing practices, their education level, or their ability to be good partners with you in supporting Adah's emerging skills, learn about the family's strengths, values, and goals.

As you learn more about each of these core considerations, you will understand how they work together and how to balance them as you plan and teach. You will begin to make decisions based on your knowledge of child development; effective educational practices; and the family, societal, and cultural values and priorities in your program's community.

Principles of Child Development and Learning

Developmentally appropriate practice is based on several principles of child and family development that have emerged from decades of research. The principles inform teachers' planning, instruction, and assessment. They also describe the importance of culture, context, and relationships for children's development.

1. Development and learning are dynamic processes that reflect the complex interplay between a child's biological characteristics and the environment, each shaping the other as well as future patterns of growth.

2. All domains of child development—physical development, cognitive development, social and emotional development, and linguistic development (including bilingual or multilingual development), as well as approaches to learning—are important; each domain both supports and is supported by the others.

3. Play promotes joyful learning that fosters self-regulation, language, cognitive, and social competencies as well as content knowledge across disciplines. Play is essential for all children, birth through age 8.

4. Although general progressions of development and learning can be identified, variations due to cultural contexts, experiences, and individual differences must also be considered.

5. Children are active learners from birth, constantly taking in and organizing information to create meaning through their relationships, their interactions with their environment, and their overall experiences.

6. Children's motivation to learn is increased when their learning environment fosters their sense of belonging, purpose, and agency. Curricula and teaching methods build on each child's assets by connecting their experiences in the school or learning environment to their home and community settings.

7. Children learn in an integrated fashion that cuts across academic disciplines or subject areas. Because the foundations of subject-area knowledge are established in early childhood, educators need subject-area knowledge, an understanding of the learning progressions within each subject area, and pedagogical knowledge about teaching each subject area's content effectively.

8. Development and learning advance when children are challenged to achieve at a level just beyond their current mastery and when they have many opportunities to reflect on and practice newly acquired skills.

9. Used responsibly and intentionally, technology and interactive media can be valuable tools for supporting children's development and learning.

Guidelines for Developmentally Appropriate Practice in Action

These three core considerations and nine principles are a foundation for six guidelines for putting developmentally appropriate practice into action. The guidelines lead teachers as they make decisions in these areas:

1. Creating a caring, equitable community of learners

2. Engaging in reciprocal partnerships with families and fostering community connections

3. Observing, documenting, and assessing children's development and learning

4. Teaching to enhance each child's development and learning

5. Planning and implementing an engaging curriculum to meaningful goals

6. Demonstrating professionalism as an early childhood educator

These guidelines are the principles in practice and form the structure of each book in the series. The star graphic below illustrates how each guideline represents one aspect of what teachers do to effectively support children's learning. Each guideline is critical to the overall practice of teachers. The guidelines all work together to create practices that are developmentally, culturally, and linguistically appropriate for all children. They are described in greater detail throughout each book.

1 Creating a Caring, Equitable Community of Learners

2 Engaging in Reciprocal Partnerships with Families and Fostering Community Connections

3 Observing, Documenting, and Assessing Children's Development and Learning

4 Teaching to Enhance Each Child's Development and Learning

5 Planning and Implementing an Engaging Curriculum to Achieve Meaningful Goals

6 Demonstrating Professionalism as an Early Childhood Educator

Developmentally Appropriate Practice with Infants and Toddlers

When you welcome an infant or toddler into your program, this child may have only weeks or months of experience in the social world outside of their family. Yet infants and toddlers are already keen observers. They are learning quickly what it means to be part of their social, emotional, linguistic, physical, and creative contexts. During times of complex change in the world, early childhood programs that are anchored in developmentally appropriate practice provide a safe and stable learning community that offers protected spaces, nurturing relationships, and rich learning environments for children to grow, thrive, and learn.

The children you teach come from unique home environments, each with its own special set of daily rituals and routines of care. Children may hear one or more languages and engage in daily interactions with multiple caregivers. Every infant and toddler develops within their own cultural contexts, and these are valuable assets to educators and to the program. Teachers attend closely to children's gazes, sounds, and movements and become careful observers of their emotions, interests, and emerging skills. They respond by preparing daily caring routines and activities that introduce children to the joy of shared exploration and learning, reading, indoor and outdoor play, music and movement, and appropriate creative and sensory experiences. When children enter your program, they will be welcomed, celebrated, and loved. They will find safe places to explore, develop positive relationships with adults and peers, and experience a sense of belonging and identity.

Families are also unique. They each have experienced a specific life journey that has led them to your program. They place immense trust in you as you teach and care for their children. They appreciate the safe and affirming relationship you offer them, where their lives and stories are valued and they are invited to contribute to decisions and participate in the life of the program. Developmentally appropriate practice provides the foundation for educators and families together to become an effective and collaborative team to nurture and teach infants and toddlers.

You are also unique. As an educator of infants and toddlers, you offer responsive, nurturing care and targeted support to the youngest, most vulnerable learners. Your own life experience and training are the starting place for self-reflection and professional growth as you apply developmentally appropriate practice to your professional journey. As you reflect with colleagues and families, you develop increasing insight about your own contexts, as well as appreciation for the experiences and contexts of others. With the framework of developmentally appropriate practice, you can use these insights to plan meaningful and joyful experiences for children.

This book invites you to discover how developmentally appropriate practice is uniquely applied to infant and toddler teaching. It highlights the six guidelines of developmentally appropriate practice and shows how, together, they provide a seamless framework of support for children's developing sense of self and others, early brain development, and language acquisition (for monolingual and dual language learners) and how this framework integrates learning in all areas through meaningful, personalized teaching. As you read about the ways other educators seek to understand the contexts of children and their families and use this knowledge in planning and decision making, you will gain valuable insights for applying this same understanding and knowledge to your own practice.

What Is in the Book?

The six parts of this book were created with you in mind. Each part highlights one of the guidelines for developmentally appropriate practice and shares how the guideline is applied to engage children and families, respond to complex challenges, and sustain joyful learning communities. The introduction to each part highlights the guideline that anchors the chapters in that section and includes overviews of each chapter. Here you'll also discover focus questions for each chapter and prompts for next steps that will help you dig deeper and apply strategies that fit within your own learning community.

The chapters reflect various facets of the guidelines, including equity, inclusion, and culturally responsive practice. The educators featured in the chapters are successfully implementing the components of the guidelines and applying developmentally appropriate practice in their work with infants and toddlers. Their real-life stories and application strategies will help you evaluate your own practice as you partner with families, colleagues, and the community to plan and prepare meaningful curriculum for children. You will be inspired to try new approaches, engage in bold conversations, and jump-start new practices for communication and teaching.

Each chapter includes sidebars (identified by an icon) that connect to one of the position statements on developmentally appropriate practice and advancing equity. Focusing on a certain aspect of developmentally appropriate practice and equity, these sidebars are intended to support your reflection on how that particular focus relates to the chapter.

Throughout the book, we note the use of the principles of child development (discussed on pages x–xi) in action to illustrate how teachers can apply what is known about child development and learning to their actual classroom practice with infants and toddlers. You will, however, want to spend some time reading more about the principles in the fourth edition of *Developmentally Appropriate Practice in Early Childhood Programs Serving Children from Birth Through Age 8*. This will give you a richer understanding of child development as you consider what is best for all the children and for each specific child, using the *both/and* thinking that is the hallmark of developmentally appropriate practice.

Part 1: Creating a Caring, Equitable Community of Learners

features stories from classroom communities centered on care and equity and grounded in nurturing, meaningful relationships. For infants and toddlers, the first communities outside of the home are extremely influential in development. To create an equitable community of learners, educators make sure that each member is valued for the strengths they bring and for their contributions to physical, psychological, and learning environments that are conductive to the learning and well-being of all. The chapters in this part showcase strategies to support healthy brain development through caring, responsive relationships. The educators also reflect on their ideas and practices to combat bias and promote belonging and inclusion. In addition, you will read about how educators address and remove bias by honoring and including family contributions. You will see how educators use physical, psychological, and learning environments to foster social and emotional learning and include families as advocates to create caring, equitable communities.

Part 2: Engaging in Reciprocal Partnerships with Families and Fostering Community Connections

digs deep into principles and strategies for building strong, respectful, two-way family-teacher relationships. It shows how the strengths and assets of families and the contexts of their communities, languages, and cultures are essential foundations for infants' and toddlers' developing sense of identity as they explore and learn. Through reciprocal partnerships, programs offer families multiple opportunities to provide information about infants' emerging development and toddlers' current explorations and interests, weigh in on decisions, share their preferences and concerns, and participate in day-to-day activities. Educators build connections with the community as a resource to strengthen program impact. In this part, you will see family engagement practices that honor family stories and invite safe and equitable communication. You will discover many ways to collaborate with families to advocate for children in the program and community, share coordinated support for development and learning, use strengths-based and trauma-informed practices to address early adversity and stress, and employ culturally aligned teaching approaches.

Part 3: Observing, Documenting, and Assessing Children's Development and Learning

invites teachers to consider the benefits of consistent, intentional observation of infants and toddlers. In this part, you will read about the ways that observation contributes to assessment and helps teachers support and scaffold children's growth and development across all developmental domains. Educators use observation, documentation, and assessment strategies to learn about children. They use what they learn to plan learning experiences that match and build on the cultural and linguistic strengths of children. Strategic planning and reflection with colleagues and families ensures high expectations and individualized support for each child. By observing infants and toddlers, educators develop a deep appreciation for children's abilities and their ways of being, thinking, and relating to others. In this part, you will read about intentional and reflective practice, using observation and documentation to include creativity and personalization in planning. You will see how educators use strengths-based, individualized scaffolding to support each child's unique paths of development and safe experiences to learn about themselves and others.

Part 4: Teaching to Enhance Each Child's Development and Learning discusses the importance of nurturing, responsive relationships with infants and toddlers as the foundation for learning and development. Developmentally appropriate teaching builds on each child's multiple assets and actively counters bias. Educators use their knowledge of each child and family to make learning experiences meaningful, accessible, and responsive to each child. They prepare the setting, schedule, and activities to support learning across all domains of development. In this part, you will find a range of creative, playful learning strategies that foster infants' discovery and engagement and that promote toddlers' active agency, curiosity, and joy in discovery and exploration. Educators use active listening and responding and provide explicit language modeling through personalized play and caring routines. They focus on cognitive growth, social and emotional skills, emergent literacy, and physical development. Educator stories in these parts share the journey of self-reflection, collaboration, and the use of anti-bias approaches to teaching.

Part 5: Planning and Implementing an Engaging Curriculum to Achieve Meaningful Goals focuses on the importance of educator knowledge of individual children, child development, and individual contexts to plan experiences that promote optimal opportunities for learning. Educators design a comprehensive curriculum that is culturally and linguistically responsive to the children and their families. Infants are introduced to songs, stories, and activities that encourage pride in their developing sense of self. Toddlers celebrate family experiences and are introduced to new people, places, and ideas. In this part, you'll see how educators connect with dual language learners and their families and encourage the development of expressive and receptive language. You'll also read about strategies to collaborate with specialists and other adults committed to children's

well-being in inclusive classrooms. Educators introduce early science and nature activities and focus on thinking skills, problem solving, cause and effect, and the importance of incorporating outdoor play.

Part 6: Demonstrating Professionalism as an Early Childhood Educator explores some of the many ways families, educators, programs, and communities work together as a coordinated network to promote quality teaching and advocate for comprehensive systems to support infant and toddler programs. Educators use the guidelines of developmentally appropriate practice, grow as professionals, and serve as informed advocates for young children and their families as well as the profession itself. In this part, you will learn about the systemic and policy supports that strengthen the workforce and professional development systems of infant and toddler teachers. You will identify important steps you can take to become an influential advocate on behalf of children, families, and your profession. Inspiring stories will help you plan your own next steps in your professional journey.

Reflection is critical to your daily practice. As you read and reread these chapters, use the reflection questions in each part's introduction to engage in conversations with colleagues and families. Consider how your work is developmentally, culturally, and linguistically appropriate for each child in your learning environment. Then use the prompts for next steps in the part introductions to act on what you learned. In what areas do you excel? What areas can be improved? How? As a lifelong learner, use the many tools and resources NAEYC offers and encourage others to do the same so that you support each and every child to achieve their full potential. To help you extend what you learn from this book, many chapters have additional material that can be accessed at NAEYC.org/books/focus-infants-toddlers. References for the book can also be found online at NAEYC.org/books/focus-infants-toddlers.

PART 1

Creating a Caring, Equitable Community of Learners

RECOMMENDATIONS FROM THE DAP STATEMENT

The foundation for the learning community is consistent, positive, caring relationships between educators and other adults and children, among children, among educators and colleagues, and between educators and families. Each member of the learning community is valued for what they bring to the community; all members are supported to consider and contribute to one another's well-being and learning.

Vera, 32 months, begins to chase Demetri (25 months) while yelling, "Demetri, Demetri!," her arms spread wide toward him. As Demetri laughs and runs away, Brian (30 months) and Peter (33 months) run after him. When Demetri drops to the floor, Brian and Peter drop down on their backs and roll around too.

Then Demetri runs to the sofa, with Brian following. When he catches up, Brian puts his arms around Demetri and leans on him. (Adapted from Recchia & Dvorakova 2018, 43)

A caring, equitable community is reflected in the welcoming spirit and warm relationships within your early childhood program. Infants and toddlers respond to the joy reflected in their educators' faces during greetings and activities. They see families and educators together celebrating their efforts and accomplishments. They learn about themselves and develop confidence in themselves in the context of the close connections between you and families. They are also beginning to build relationships among themselves, which can flourish amid the caring and safe social and play experiences you provide. These early experiences are very influential in the lives of infants and toddlers because they develop ideas about themselves and grasp their significance to others through genuine and consistent relationships.

Educators make teaching personal—getting to know each child's family, learning about their unique cultural and linguistic experiences, and using these as assets for planning and supporting children's learning. They communicate with families and colleagues and explore the community to understand the contexts of each child and to foster each child's enjoyment of and engagement in learning. Remaining attuned to daily patterns and changes in development enables teachers to adapt the environment and their support to align with the strengths and needs of each child, fostering their exploration and growth.

Teachers also provide safety, security, and emotional support to infants and toddlers through proactive and responsive caring routines. As you engage with children in these routines, listen to and acknowledge their feelings, using words as well as nonverbal means to reflect what the children are communicating. Recognize signs of stress and work closely with families to be sure children are psychologically and physically safe. Include families' home languages, cultures, and ways of interacting with their children in the setting to help make it feel familiar and safe, encouraging children to explore and play. Provide frequent opportunities for infants' and toddlers' self-directed play; active, physical movement; and joyful exploration as part of the daily schedule. Don't forget outdoor experiences! They offer interaction with the natural world to delight young children and engage their curiosity and interest.

A caring, equitable community is characterized by reflective, inclusive practices. Educators take care to reflect on their own behaviors and the ways in which these may affect children's developing sense of personal identity, self-agency, and self-worth, knowing that implicit biases can interfere with children's well-being and learning. Children with and without disabilities feel that they are valued when you guide activities and routines with gentleness, encouragement, and respect and build on their contributions and assets through strengths-based teaching. In such an environment, children learn *from* and *with* each other.

The chapters in Part 1 showcase authors who create spaces where children and families experience safety, equity, and inclusion. Like you, these teachers hold deep respect for the patterns of life, routines, and practices of families, and they explore ways they can support each child's security and sense of belonging.

READ AND REFLECT

As you read the chapters in this section, consider and evaluate your own classroom practices using these reflection questions.

"Caring Relationships: The Heart of Early Brain Development" presents the positive impact of caregivers' responsiveness and consistency on the brain development of infants and toddlers. Understanding this, teachers can identify and use strategies that are in harmony with the developing brain and build a solid foundation for learning. **Consider:** How do the caring routines you use impact a child's developing sense of self? How do your interactions during play, routines, and meals offer opportunities for language development and learning?

"Care and Equity in Toddler Classrooms: Practices for Creating, Sustaining, and Empowering Community" illustrates ways teachers can facilitate collaborative spaces where families are full partners in contributing to joyful learning in a toddler classroom. **Consider:** In what ways does your program invite families to participate in daily program life? How do you include families who are not able to be physically present in the program? How do you show appreciation for the contributions that families make to the program?

"Cultivating Positive Relationships and Physical Environments to Support Emotional Well-Being" illustrates how infant and toddler development is impacted by cultural, social and emotional, and physical contexts. Learning about children's unique family experiences enables you to respond to children's strengths, assets, and needs. **Consider:** How do you connect with families so that they feel safe sharing their personal experiences? What approaches do you use with children and families who are currently experiencing loss, grief, and other traumatic experiences? What community resources are available for you and families to explore together?

"The First Step for Addressing Bias in Infant and Toddler Programs" invites you to discover insights about the roots of bias and find strategies for increasing sensitivity, compassion, and understanding of yourself and others. Through shared reflection, you can design experiences that promote a sense of belonging and of being valued for each member. **Consider:** Think about the ideas you hold about early caregiving routines and interactions. What practices do you think are important? How might

your ideas differ from those of the families in your program? How can you challenge yourself and think about situations in new ways as you consider what is in children's best interests?

NEXT STEPS

You'll find many ideas and strategies in these chapters that you can integrate into your work to support children and their families. As you read, remember that the caring community you are creating is special and unique to your setting. Then consider the following suggestions as you plan next steps.

1. Identify at least two practices you learn from these chapters that may be most effective with the infants and toddlers you teach. Try them out and share your observations with a colleague.

2. Talk with a coach or colleague about ways to create a more inclusive, culturally responsive, personally safe, and encouraging community for those you work with. What is already working well? In what areas would you like to make changes, and how would these impact your practice? Identify two specific changes you could make and implement them.

3. Identify and carry out a new strategy to connect with families and learn about their stories and experiences. Note the ways listening to families challenges your own thinking. How does learning about the contexts and strengths of families help you become more intentional in creating culturally responsive experiences for children?

References for the chapters in this part can be accessed online at NAEYC.org/books/focus-infants-toddlers.

CHAPTER 1

Caring Relationships
The Heart of Early Brain Development

J. Ronald Lally and Peter L. Mangione

Of all that brain science has taught us over the last 30 years, one of the clearest findings is that early brain development is directly influenced by infants' day-to-day interactions with their caregivers. Even before birth, babies have a built-in expectation that adults will be available and care for their needs (Shonkoff & Phillips 2000). Their very survival depends on this availability. If babies' expectations for protection and nurturance are met, their brains experience pleasure and delight. These pleasurable early interactions stimulate the brain, motivating the baby to relate to those who care for them with confidence and ease. If their expectations are less than adequately met, their confidence in getting their needs met through relationships may be challenged. When this occurs, emotional and social development suffer, and because babies' emotional base is the foundation for all other learning, so do intellectual and language development (Center on the Developing Child 2016; IOM & NRC 2015).

Authors' Note

In this chapter, we use the term *caregivers* to refer to all adults who care for and teach young children, including family members, family child care providers, and all early childhood educators.

A baby's early experiences in relationships, whether at home or in an early learning environment, set the stage for future brain functioning. The information gathered in these early relationships is at the heart of a rich and complex brain-building process. As infants experience responses from their caregivers, their brains start to form expectations for how they will be treated and how they should respond. For example, when a baby fusses or cries, consistent adult responses that provide comfort help the child anticipate similar responses

in the future. As the expectations are strengthened by similar experiences being repeated, babies' brains construct perceptions of the social and emotional world in which they live. Those perceptions influence how infants understand their environment, relate to others, and engage in learning.

When those experiences are primarily positive, children perceive the behaviors and messages of others in positive ways and are motivated to explore more and more of the world (including people and objects). When babies have repeated adverse early experiences, they come to expect the behaviors and messages of others to be negative, and they start to perceive new experiences with others in a negative way. In early brain growth, experience creates expectation, which alters perception.

Whether infants' early relationships are largely positive or negative significantly impacts their ability to manage stress. From birth to age 3, stress can have an especially adverse effect on brain development (IOM & NRC 2015). When children have positive early relationship experiences, they develop emotionally secure attachments with their caregivers that can buffer stress at various levels of intensity. Stress that is severe and persistent becomes toxic, and the emotional buffers provided by secure relationships are even more crucially important (Center on the Developing Child 2016). When children have to cope with tolerable (less intense and temporary) stress, emotionally secure relationships help children regulate their responses and, once the stress subsides, refocus on exploration and learning. What we have learned from brain research in the last 30 years is that the "tender loving care" advocated by early childhood educators for many decades is not only the kind way to treat children but a crucial part of early brain development.

Healthy Early Brain Development from Birth to Age 3

During the first three years of life, children go through a period of "prolonged helplessness," dependent on others for safety, survival, and socialization (Gopnik 2016). Because babies' brains are programmed to learn from their caregivers, this period of helplessness is a strength, not a weakness. Infants' and toddlers' time with others wires their brains for survival in anticipation of future functioning (Gopnik 2016). The brain builds crucial structures and pathways that serve as the foundation for future social, emotional, language, and intellectual functioning (Drury et al. 2010; Meltzoff & Kuhl 2016; Schore 2005). Therefore, the relationships a child experiences each day and the environments in which those relationships play out are the building blocks of the brain. By participating in learning experiences with their caregivers, babies' brains develop to function in the particular physical, social, cultural, and linguistic environments of those who care for them. Infants learn, largely by attending to their caregivers' modeling, how to feel, think, and act. Simple, daily interactions have an enormous impact. For example, a caregiver who performs routines in a gentle way and uses language to help the child anticipate what will happen next teaches the child to learn about caring relationships and supports language development. During this formative period, it is critically important for caregivers to create a climate of care with healthy brain growth in mind. Simply stated, young children develop and function well when provided care in safe, interesting, and intimate settings where they establish and sustain secure and trusting relationships with knowledgeable caregivers who are responsive to their needs and interests (Lally 2006; Mangione et al. 2021).

The infant brain is at once vulnerable and competent; both of these attributes need to be addressed simultaneously for healthy brain development. The vulnerable baby is dependent on relationships with adults for physical survival, emotional security, a safe base for learning, help with self-regulation, modeling and mentoring social behavior, and information and exchanges about the workings of the world and rules for living. Yet at the same time, the infant comes into the world with great competence as a curious, motivated, self-starting learner—an imitator, interpreter, integrator, inventor, explorer, communicator, meaning seeker, and relationship builder. For the brain to grow robustly, it needs a context of caring relationships that simultaneously provide emotional predictability for the baby's vulnerable side and a climate of intellectual novelty for the competent side (Lally 2013).

Birth to 9 Months: Caring Relationships and the Brain During the Attachment Period

During the first stage of development outside the womb, much of babies' initial attention focuses on forming and strengthening secure connections with their caregivers. Rather than passively receiving care, babies actively seek it out. They come into the world with physical skills and social competences that prepare them to play an active role in their development. They are wired to react to those around them in ways that elicit interest and increase the likelihood of contact and closeness (Marvin & Britner 2008; Wittmer & Honig 2020). Based on the feedback infants receive from early exchanges, they direct attachment behaviors toward developing secure relationships with their primary caregivers.

Research has shown that this attachment-seeking fits with the finding that during the first two years of brain development, emotional wiring is the dominant activity. The brain builds crucial structures and pathways of emotional functioning that serve as the base for attachment, future emotional and social activity, and the language and intellectual development that will follow (Center on the Developing Child 2016; Schore 2000). In this earliest stage, babies start using messages from caregivers to develop perceptions of the extent to which they are loved. Infants then use these perceptions to create an initial working model for how to engage with others. Thus, the care babies receive during these early exchanges directly affects the quality of attachment they form with their caregivers and influences the emotional stance they will take in interactions with others.

> Young babies need relationships with caregivers who are
>
> › Sensitive to their needs and messages
>
> › Timely in responding (especially to messages of distress)
>
> › Accurate in the reading of their cues
>
> › Understanding of appropriate levels of stimulation (Bornstein 2012)

Seven to 18 Months: Caring Relationships and the Brain During the Exploration Stage

Between 7 and 18 months of age, babies have a natural drive to explore their local environment, objects, and people; develop a basic understanding of themselves; and test the strength and use of relationships. Using their emerging motor skills to explore, they venture from the safety of the physical closeness of their caregivers and test the strength of relationships. They come and go while carefully observing their caregiver's attentiveness and emotional availability. They are, in a sense, practicing independence (Eisenberg, Hofer, & Vaughan 2007). Also at this stage, babies' brains are preparing for a life that does not revolve entirely around physical proximity to their caregiver. Based on their caregivers' reactions to their actions, infants and toddlers begin to hold in mind lessons learned, such as which independent explorations are considered socially appropriate and which are not, and what activities are dangerous, like playing near an ungated stairway.

EQUITY Toxic stress disproportionately affects children of marginalized groups. Effective teachers offer positive, secure relationships and equitable, high-quality learning opportunities that build on each child's individual and family strengths.

Babies' communication and language skills increase dramatically during the exploration stage. Although babies can say only a few words, they come to understand many more (IOM & NRC 2015; Thompson 2011). The words they hear from adults stimulate the language development pathways in the brain. It is not only the words that matter, but also the larger patterns of communication—not just what is said, but how it is said and received (Pawl & St. John 1998). After repeated exchanges with their caregivers, infants start to build a primitive sense of self. They come to expect the following:

› "I am listened to or not."

› "What I choose to do is valued or isn't."

› "How I express my emotions is accepted or isn't."

› "I am allowed to explore or not."

› "Mostly my needs are met or not."

The thoughts, emotions, and shared experiences that the developing brain processes in interactions with adults have a profound impact on the developing child's self-perception and actions.

Fifteen to 36 Months: Caring Relationships and the Brain During the Self-Definition Stage

During the third stage, young children are developing an awareness of their separateness from their caregivers and peers as well as a sense of themselves as individuals (O'Shaughnessy et al. 2023). They begin to exhibit self-conscious emotions, are particularly sensitive to others' judgments, feel shame and embarrassment easily when others critique their behaviors and appearance, and start to develop a conscience.

This stage is also characterized by an explosion of brain growth in several areas of development (in addition to the emotional development that was dominant earlier). Intellectually, children hold ideas in their minds briefly, engage in pretend play, and become increasingly able to focus their attention on topics, people, and objects introduced by others. Their use of spoken language increases greatly. They use many new words and complex sentence structures. Children develop perceptual and motor skills that allow them to run fast, climb high, and hit hard—making the development of self-control especially important (Brownell & Kopp 2007).

Fortunately, this self-definition stage also brings the early emergence of executive function skills, which include the development of working memory, mental flexibility, and self-control (Center on the Developing Child 2012). These emerging skills influence all areas of development, increasing children's capacity to explore and learn about their social environment—and to navigate conflicts with others. As children gain a clearer understanding of independent, separate interests, they realize they have choices, which is quite liberating.

Promoting Brain Development During Caring Routines and Teaching

Care that offers predictable routines in safe, clearly defined environments; respectful, responsive interactions; and consistent positive guidance strengthens self-regulation and the beginnings of executive function. The following resources offer additional information about promoting brain development during caring routines and teaching:

> Center on the Developing Child at Harvard University, Brain Building Through Play—Activities for Infants, Toddlers, and Children. https:// developingchild.harvard.edu/resources/ brainbuildingthroughplay

> Early Childhood Learning and Knowledge Center, Supporting Early Brain Development—Building the Brain. https://eclkc.ohs.acf.hhs.gov/ publication/supporting-early-brain-development-building-brain

> Zero to Three, Early Brain Development. www.zerotothree.org/early-brain-development

However, with choices—particularly those involving caregivers and peers—comes a dawning awareness of responsibility. This choice-responsibility tension is central to the drama of this stage. Once again, caring relationships play a prominent role in how the young brain becomes structured. How adults react during this tension-filled period of life greatly affects how young children come to see their rights and others' rights.

Interactions children have with their caregivers, peers, and others shape their brains' social and emotional future. What toddlers experience in their day-to-day lives forms their expectations for what constitutes appropriate behavior toward others (Barry & Kochanska 2010; IOM & NRC 2015). These early experiences provide lessons for developing moral and ethical codes, gaining control of impulses and emotions, and learning and adapting to the rules of their family, culture, and society. As young children experience a growing sense of independence and self-control, their brains' capacity to regulate their behavior continues to develop; however, they still need guidance from adults, and this guidance most often comes through caring relationships.

A child's young brain needs adults to act in ways that honor the child's rights to desire, hope, explore, and show preferences, while also helping the child learn to honor the similar rights of others. Although the child is growing older and more independent, the young brain remains vulnerable. Caring relationships, with clear rules for behavior that are consistently applied in reasoned ways, provide safety while the brain is still being formed, ensuring that individuation experiences and socialization lessons occur in a fair and predictable environment.

Creating a Positive Climate of Care with Healthy Brain Growth in Mind

Support each child's sense of security, joy, love of learning, and shared relationships by using intentional strategies to boost learning. Here are some steps to connect with and nurture infants' and toddlers' growth:

> **Be a keen observer.** Ask yourself questions to be responsive and guide your planning. When and in what situations do the children seek attention? With whom and with what do they prefer to play? How do they communicate that they are delighted, enthusiastic, or ready for a challenge? What signs indicate that they are overstimulated, tired, hungry, bored, or need a change of pace? How can you respond to these cues to support children's emotional security, learning, and well-being?

> **Create consistency.** Learn from families about feeding preferences, toileting practices, and sleeping routines. Incorporate what you learn to create consistency between home and the program.

> **Offer choices.** Plan environments, interactions, and routines that engage and connect with children's growth and development. Offer play materials to engage children's interests, balance familiarity with novelty, and provide a range of challenges and choices.

> **Build on children's interests.** Notice when infants and toddlers show excitement about a play material, idea, or activity and consider ways to extend their interest. If they are fascinated by birds at the feeder, possible ways to extend their interest include adding picture books, songs, and finger plays about birds.

> **Use words to connect ideas and experiences.** Consistently engage in conversation with children and model language throughout the day. When a child shows interest in something and is attentive, use words that connect with the child's interest. For example, when the child is patting a stuffed animal: "The bunny is soft and smooth. What do his ears feel like?" While playing a tube game: "The ball makes a swishing sound when it rolls down the tube. What a funny sound. Everyone laughs when they hear it."

> **Integrate music into the children's daily experience.** Enjoy finger plays, puppets, rhyming songs, and music and movement to encourage playfulness with language, body awareness, and shared activity.

> **Spend time giving full attention to each child.** Make eye contact and engage in conversations with individual children during meals, other care routines, and play. For example, while reading "What happens when you take a bath like Little Rabbit? How does your momma wash your hair?"

Conclusion

What we are learning from brain science helps us better understand the multiple factors that influence young children's development and provides us with caregiving and teaching strategies that are in harmony with the developing brain. In essence, brain development is about the whole child in context, from the health of the mother to the child's early experiences in the culture and language of their family, their community, and their early learning program. The foundation of brain development is social and emotional development grounded in caring relationships. If caregivers are mindful of how a child's whole experience—particularly the emotional tenor—influences the developing brain, they can provide caring relationships that help the child feel secure and open up to an engaging world of exploration and learning throughout the early years.

J. RONALD LALLY, EdD, was one of the pioneers in the field of infant and toddler development and was the codirector of the Center for Child and Family Studies at WestEd, a research development and service agency.

PETER L. MANGIONE, PhD, is director of early childhood strategic initiatives at WestEd. He previously was codirector of the Center for Child and Family Studies at WestEd. Peter codirected and now directs the Program for Infant/Toddler Care.

CHAPTER 2

Care and Equity in Toddler Classrooms

Practices for Creating, Sustaining, and Empowering Community

Nana E. Appiah-Korang and Abigail P. Gulden

Equity in early childhood programs means, in part, "viewing each child as an individual" and creating a space where "children see themselves and each other—their social and cultural identities—reflected and respected" (Wright 2022, 112). It also means that teachers provide each child with what they need to thrive and that they support families to feel seen, empowered, and celebrated within the classroom and beyond. Therefore, supporting equity as an educator through creating a caring community of learners involves a few things: carefully observing the children, intentionally documenting their growth, and using these observations and documentations to highlight and invite participation from families and communities of origin. In this chapter, we explore how we have honored and included families and their funds of knowledge through our documentation in our classrooms (Nana with 1-year-olds turning 2 and Perry with 2-year-olds turning 3) in the pursuit of a caring and equitable community.

Observation and Documentation: Foundational Knowing

In my (Nana) classroom of toddlers, observing is one of the things I enjoy doing the most. It allows me to see, hear, and know more about each child as an individual and also about the whole group, which is critical with infants and toddlers, as many are just beginning to communicate verbally. Documenting your observations of children is also one way to build on each child's funds of knowledge—the knowledge children possess and come to school with based on their home and family experiences (McWayne et al. 2020; Moll et al. 1992). Take, for example, a toddler diapering a baby doll in the dramatic play area, which she has watched her family doing numerous times and has a keen interest in. When I observe this child, I might gain insight into the child's frustration level or their ability to persevere or problem solve. Over time, using information gathered from repeated observations of this child and documentation of their explorations and narration of their actions, I understand more about the trajectory of the child's growth in developing this skill and gain a sense of when and how to offer support as well as when to step back. While it's crucial to understand children's current knowledge and skills, it is also important to use documentation to assist them in expanding their knowledge and skills.

Supporting Individual Strengths Through Documentation and Sharing

Throughout the year, as we devote time to observing and documenting children's engagement and learning, we have opportunities to see how they prefer to interact with classroom materials and how they demonstrate their learning and strengths. With this knowledge, we can effectively differentiate learning experiences in the classroom, providing each child with the appropriate support based on

their development, interests, and needs. It is a joy to give space to individual children to lean into their strengths, to watch as they model those strengths for others, and to observe children as they display their competence for their classmates. As an example, one year a child mastered the skill of diapering a doll in the dramatic play area, and we photographed her steps and displayed them with her quotes in the area (e.g., "Put the baby on his back") as documentation of one way to diaper a doll (see the photograph). Afterward, we noticed that she would offer assistance to her peers when she saw them following her steps.

Eventually, we repeated this same sequence in all the different learning areas at different times in our classroom. Eventually our walls became filled with

documentation showcasing each child's learning. We observed that children enjoyed pointing out and asking questions about what they and their peers were doing in the documentation display. They asked questions such as "What is Steve doing to the plant?" and "Can I water the plant too?" Other times, they simply pointed at a picture and said, "Steve!" In this engagement, we saw how children both valued the thoughts of their peers and applied them to their own work, identifying ways that they might build on their own strengths and assets. I am grateful that my school allows teachers the time and space to document these experiences and encourages us to make documentation available to the children so that they can feel seen, valued, and validated.

Recognizing children's unique expertise and abilities dovetails with providing them opportunities to connect with each other. For example, in the wintertime, putting on and taking off layers of clothing becomes a curriculum in and of itself for toddlers. We encourage children who are more experienced to lend a hand to their peers, creating a community where power and know-how is distributed between teachers and children. However, creating a caring and equitable community of learners involves going beyond illuminating particular strengths. It also involves reflecting on the identities that children carry into and outside of the classroom.

Embracing Identity Exploration in the Curriculum: A Study of Self

To foster a caring community, educators must cultivate children's curiosity about, empathy toward, and interest in one another (Derman-Sparks & Edwards, with Goins 2020; Wright 2022). In my (Perry) classroom of older toddlers, one of the grounding explorations we conduct throughout the year is an extended study of self. Over the year, as teachers increasingly see and understand individual children, we invite the children to dive into explorations about how they are seen by families, themselves, and each other.

This past year, we began this exploration by inviting the children to create self-portraits using loose parts (buttons, wire, gems, and so on) and clay. A week later, we explored skin tone using paint and 10 shades of playdough that I mixed at home. Next, we revisited the children's self-portraits: first with black pens and paper and then in a variety of forms, acknowledging that there are multiple "languages" children may wish to use to create (Edwards, Gandini, & Forman 2012). Each of these explorations revealed a new dimension of the children to us, showing us a way that children saw themselves and, perhaps, how they wished to be seen by the world.

 DAP By observing and participating in the community, children learn about themselves, their world, and how to develop positive, constructive relationships with other people.

The study of self is an essential piece of our school's toddler curriculum. Toddlers are people who are often not seen as whole individuals quite yet, but in fact they are independent, capable citizens who often see themselves more clearly than adults do. Embracing toddlers' abilities by inviting them to create representations of themselves is an empowering experience for children and can support their developing sense of confidence in their classroom community. However, as educators we also desire to support children's confidence beyond the classroom, in their homes, communities, and families. In the next section we turn our attention to some of the ways that we have invited and encouraged family participation in the program. In some of the stories, you'll also see how documentation remained an important part of this work.

Practices for Supporting a Caring and Equitable Learning Community

A few practices are especially important when creating a caring and equitable community of learners with toddlers.

> Teachers facilitate caring and equitable communities when they view classrooms as collaborative spaces. Use phrases such as "our classroom" (instead of "my classroom") and "We are a team." Collaborative language communicates that adults are community members alongside the children.

> Teachers understand and model that everyone brings unique strengths and abilities to the community. For example, when Lucy asks for help opening her snack, I suggest she ask Freddy, who is great at opening things. While Freddy has a hard time sitting during snack time, he benefits from opportunities to help others.

> Teachers explicitly invite families to share information about their lives, their children, and other important aspects of their experiences. Bring families' voices into the classroom and the curriculum through written responses and in-person conversation.

> Teachers make use of micro-moments of connection with families—the brief instances where a kind word or interesting insight can be listened to and/or shared. A micro-moment can take place at drop-off or pickup, in a quick conversation at a family event, or even in an email exchange. For example, a parent once shared that their child had been asking about different types of trees on the walk to school; I responded that we had recently read a book about trees. This let me know the child had a desire to dive deeper into this topic both at home and school. As a result, I planned walks around the neighborhood and invited a parent expert to help us identify the types of trees we saw.

> Rather than overlook different views about teaching, teachers take time to verbalize and discuss their experiences and ideas. For example, after observing a teacher rushing to get the children outside to the playground by zipping their coats instead of allowing them to do it themselves, a colleague suggested making more time in the schedule for the children to get ready for the playground so that they could practice their independence.

> Teachers seek not to bury differences in people but to verbalize and discuss them. For example, teachers take time to highlight differences and educate children about the special rights (the term we use in place of *special needs* or *disabilities*), languages, and cultures represented by families in the program and others in the community.

Valuing Family Strengths

Another essential piece of creating a caring and equitable community involves connecting with families. Families are, often for the first time, entrusting their child's care to individuals outside of their immediate circles of family and friends. It is our role as educators to invite families to share their particular social and cultural and social funds of knowledge with the classroom community. At the start of each year, our school's classes send out a family questionnaire to gather information on family background, composition, rituals, and routines. This survey, in addition to conversations at pickup and drop-off times, email exchanges, and so on, supports us in developing strong foundational relationships with families that we build on over the course of the year and use to support and enrich our community.

Family members of all students in our program also have the option to do what we term "classroom helping," in which they are invited to spend the day with us and participate in the classroom. Families can volunteer in the classroom as much or as little as their schedule allows, which means that some children have a classroom helper more frequently than other peers. All classroom helpers, however, find ways to make their child's peers feel special too, further helping to build a sense of community.

Enriching the Curriculum with Families' Contributions

The information we learn about the children, their families, and their experiences—through the activities mentioned above, the questionnaire, and informal conversations during classroom helping—allows us to support, inform, and expand curriculum and daily activities. It also fosters community within our classroom. Without fail, we find that each family has something unique that makes them special and that we can learn and grow from as a group—strengths and assets that we can tap into during specific projects or curriculum threads.

For example, when the children displayed an interest in airplane dramatic play, my coteacher and I were excited. We played for a few weeks and began building a plane. Ida's dad, an engineer, suggested we add a movable wing to the airplane we had built. Ida was thrilled when her dad climbed into the loft with her and the two of them hammered and constructed what he envisioned. After noticing that the airplane play seemed to be enduring, we decided to draw on Diego's family's knowledge and skills, as Diego's father is an airline pilot. We asked Antonio to visit our classroom dressed in his pilot uniform. When he visited, Antonio showed us a control board made from recycled materials (that he had made at home!) that mirrored the ones found in planes. The children also had an opportunity to ask Antonio a list of questions they'd prepared with teacher support. Each of these families built on one another's knowledge and supported our class in becoming a collaborative community even across time and space.

Having family members use their expertise to extend curriculum through spending time with their child's peers enriches a classroom in many ways. Each child who shares their family's funds of knowledge enjoys a new opportunity to connect more deeply with their peers and teachers, which empowers and reaffirms the child in their family of origin. Take, for example, Isabelle's story below.

> Our sensory table tube that drains the water is clogged. It doesn't have a cap at the top, meaning that materials enter the tube and get stuck. My coteacher and I have tried a couple of different things to plug the hole early on in the year but have been unsuccessful. A few months in, Isabelle's mother is visiting and notices me pouring the water out by lifting the entire table and dumping it into a bucket. She asks why we don't use the tube to drain it, and we tell her our issue. After asking if she can help—to which we readily reply, "Absolutely"—she takes a closer look and eventually figures out how to remove the hose and unclog the drain. While the table still needs a cover to keep the water in, it feels so good to have the drain unclogged.

> The next day, 3-year-old Isabelle arrives at school with a bag from the hardware store. The bag is filled with different parts for us to try to cover the drain. All the children gather around the sensory table as we try the various sized parts until we find the perfect fit and plug the drain. Isabelle is especially excited and proud of this moment.

This story provides an important reminder that bringing in family funds of knowledge to create an equitable community can be as simple as inviting a family member to use their knowledge and time to contribute to something physical within the classroom space. This experience acknowledges the potential constraints on time that families have and recognizes their unique skills. It also allows children to see their families involved, and to become involved themselves, in the classroom operations. Isabelle was so proud that her mom was the one who sent in the tools to fix the sensory table. Her experience and that of her family was directly reflected in the classroom.

Embracing Families' Cultures in Meaningful Ways

Families also bring culture into the classroom, often in creative ways, when teachers make space for it, welcoming and celebrating it. The experience relayed below was repeated with the same family in two different schools and with two different age groups. In each of these settings, I (Nana) and my coteacher worked with the family to share a special tradition and knowledge that benefited the classroom community.

> While student teaching at a university early childhood learning lab, I (Nana) had witnessed a Korean mother leading a morning meeting. She has been invited by the lead teachers to share something about Hangul Day, the celebration of the Korean alphabet. As one of the activities, she worked with each child to write their name in Korean.

> Some years later, when another of her children is a student in my class, I share how much I enjoyed and appreciated her presentation. To my delight,

she offers to do the same thing again. For weeks, my coteacher and I work with her to translate her presentation for toddlers. Rather than write the children's names in Korean, the mother brings in Korean alphabet magnets to explore with the children. She also brings a Hangul alphabet puzzle, which is extremely popular with the children. They are intrigued by a Hangul scroll that reveals black ink when it comes into contact with water. The mother brings in some Korean books as well. Of course, toddlers are not yet reading words or necessarily identifying letters; however, the children very much enjoy flipping through the books, noticing and commenting on the features of the letters of the Korean alphabet and trying to piece together the story using the illustrations.

We make a point to document and share this presentation with other families in our classroom community. As the school year progresses, we observe a snowball effect where, after reading about this experience, several other families ask if they can share their own creative cultural activities with us. Over the course of the year, in addition to Hangul, we explore Diwali, learn about elements of Nigerian cultural attire, bake sourdough bread with a family, and have parents lead music sessions with various instruments.

Each of these opportunities provided a way for children to see themselves and their families reflected in the concrete daily experience of the classroom. The experiences also helped families realize that all sorts of assets and funds of knowledge are valuable and contribute meaningfully to the classroom community.

Deepening Family-School Connections

One way we try to deepen the connection between families and the classroom is by creating documentation boards in the hallways outside our classrooms that display current curriculum and children's work or photos of their experiences. (See the documentation board below for the airplane project described previously.) Often we include an interactive element, such as a question on a topic with a pen and space for handwritten answers or books to flip through that detail the process of an experience. We also send out digital or printed versions of documentation for families who are less frequently present at pickup and drop-off or school events.

While our documentation strives to bring families in, some still struggle to find and/or make time to connect. Acknowledging and integrating family strengths has to be done in a way that shows that we respect their time and respond to the busyness families feel without overwhelming them. For example, we share children's work briefly at drop-off or pickup times and follow up later on with an email that provides more information.

interests, and funds of knowledge. This involves close, intentional observation as well as a concerted effort to build and sustain relationships with families, providing multiple, varied opportunities for them to share their interests, abilities, and knowledge with our classroom community.

Foremost, we celebrate them!

NANA E. APPIAH-KORANG, MEd, works as one of the lead infant and toddler teachers at Newtowne School in Cambridge, Massachusetts. She holds a master's degree in early childhood education from Boston University.

ABIGAIL PERRY GULDEN, BA, has been teaching in Reggio-inspired toddler classrooms in Greater Boston for five years. She is currently pursuing a master's degree in early childhood education.

While all families care deeply for their children, many families are still building an understanding of the idea that fostering a climate of equity and care is possible in spaces dedicated to the development of very young children. Many are unfamiliar with exactly how this might look. There are times when a parent or caregiver may make comments or ask questions about other children's differences. These moments, while sometimes uncomfortable, are also opportunities to demonstrate that our goal is to provide a safe, nurturing space for all children. I often use the phrase "Everyone is working on something different in our classroom" to remind children *and* adults that everyone has strengths as well as things they are still learning. This is what makes our community special and also more fun!

Conclusion

Children have multiple identities and show up, each day, bringing all of them into our community. This means that our classrooms are diverse linguistically, ethnically, and intrapersonally, and by documenting these differences we have an opportunity to reveal them for what they really are—strengths and assets for our community. Every child enjoys different things; every child brings a unique temperament to their interactions; and every child engages with their surroundings differently, influenced by their own unique experiences. In our classroom, we strive to respond to each child based on their own personality,

Cultivating Positive Relationships and Physical Environments to Support Emotional Well-Being

Iheoma U. Iruka

Joshua, a 2-year-old in Ms. Keller's class, has been staying at a family friend's house because of his father's depression since Joshua's mother died during childbirth. Ms. Keller has known Joshua's father for many years since they both grew up in the community. She knows about the deep loss the family has experienced and that Joshua is now staying with a family friend.

On many days, Joshua stays close to his teacher and avoids the other children, pushing them away or swatting at those who approach him. Ms. Keller recognizes that he needs consistency and assurance that he is cared for and safe. She understands that building a caring, consistent relationship with Joshua provides a buffering effect against trauma, helping Joshua to overcome adverse experiences and promote healthy, secure learning and development. Ms. Keller provides Joshua with a blanket that he keeps at the center to hold when he is upset. She makes time to do one-on-one activities with him, like reading his favorite book while rubbing his hands. She has also found that singing and dancing to "Shake Your Sillies Out" with Joshua and another child he likes really gets him energized for the day.

To help Joshua and other children in the class understand their own and others' emotions, Ms. Keller provides words to describe their feelings as they are experiencing them: "You look sad that we have to clean up" or "You are mad because Ella took your truck." Ms. Keller always tries to acknowledge each child's emotion and offer an action: "Joshua is feeling sad. Let's find a book about feeling sad" or "Jamal, Joshua feels sad. Can he sit next to you to play with the trucks?"

This example illustrates the importance of positive relationships to a child's development. Joshua is experiencing many significant stressors, including the loss of his mother and living away from his father for a period of time. Understandably, he sometimes exhibits strong emotions. His teacher adjusts her approach to support a child she knows is under stress. The connections among the learning environment, the circumstances in which Joshua lives, and his emotions require Ms. Keller to make intentional decisions to spend more one-on-one time with Joshua, select materials and activities that help him feel safe, and model some approaches he can use to regulate his own emotions. She understands that building a relationship with him that provides him with a feeling of security is critical to his development.

Ms. Keller knew a lot about Joshua's home experience and background and understood some of the causes of his stress. However, you may not always be aware of the cause of a child's emotions or behavior. To support a child who appears to be experiencing stress and sadness, you may need to reach out to the family to find out background information for a fuller understanding. While you may not always have the opportunity to engage in focused one-on-one interactions with the child, you may be able to engage other children in supporting their peer, as Ms. Keller did when she asked Jamal if Joshua could sit near him as they played with trucks. Children are often eager to help cheer up a friend who seems sad.

The Importance of Relationships and the Environment to Learning

Evolving research in multiple disciplines offers new insights into the importance of the early years in children's learning and development. The development of the brain and other biological systems impacts a child's ability to learn and is heavily influenced by environmental factors (NASEM 2016, 2019). Environmental factors that affect development include cultural (e.g., feeding and toileting practices), social and emotional (e.g., adult interactions with and responses to children), and physical influences (e.g., sleep, nutrition, and exposure to chemical substances such as lead).

Biological and environmental factors interact in myriad complex ways that impact children's development: "All biological systems in the body interact with each other and adapt to the contexts in which a child is developing—for better or for worse—and adaptations in one system can influence adaptations in others" (National Scientific Council on the Developing Child 2020, 2).

Particularly for children experiencing stress, factors such as reducing long-term stressors; having strong, caring, and positive relationships; and developing key life skills have a profound impact on supporting young children's learning:

> Learning is a dynamic, ongoing process that is simultaneously biological and cultural. Attention to both individual factors (such as developmental stage; physical, emotional, and mental health; and interests and motivations), as well as factors external to the individual (such as the environment in which the learner is situated, social and cultural contexts, and opportunities available to learners) is necessary to develop a complete picture of the nature of learning. (NASEM 2018, 26)

Creating an Environment to Mitigate the Effects of Stress and Trauma

It is important to understand how environmental factors such as consistent, sensitive, and responsive caregiving and close child-adult relationships can lead to positive childhood experiences. Likewise, it is important to recognize the effects that trauma and adverse childhood experiences (ACEs) have on child development.

DAP Observing carefully to identify the stress and sadness that infants and toddlers experience—and being aware of the buffering effects of caring, consistent relationships—can help teachers calm and support children when they are worried, afraid, or anxious.

The environments that early childhood educators create offer a foundation for supporting positive relationships and experiences with children and for protecting them from stress and trauma. Consider this example in the earliest years of a child's life:

> When adults are sensitive and respond to an infant's babble, cry, or gesture, they directly support the development of neural connections that lay the foundation for children's communication and social skills, including self-regulation. These "serve and return" interactions shape the brain's architecture. They also help educators and others "tune in" to the infant and better respond to the infant's wants and needs. (NAEYC 2020a, 8)

Arranging a physical environment that meets children's individual physical, social and emotional, and learning needs conveys to children of all ages that they are safe, valued, supported, capable, and resilient (Erdman & Colker, with Winter 2020; Iruka et al. 2023)—all of which contribute to children's ability to trust others and focus on learning.

Strategies to Support Children Through Long-Term Stress

by Marie Masterson

During prolonged times of financial difficulties, illness, community trauma, and crisis, teachers need effective strategies to calm and comfort children. Here are some suggestions.

> Notice signs of stress, such as a change in behavior, crying, prolonged quietness, or anxiety.

> Reassure children through gentle physical responses, words, and tone of voice.

> Ensure that adults model calm and soothing reactions.

> Keep a predictable schedule of caring routines to develop trust.

> Offer a lovey, blanket, or pacifier when part of the family's guidance.

> Monitor levels of stimulation and offer quiet and soft spaces.

> Provide soft and soothing sensory experiences, such as water and sand-type play.

> Enjoy lap time or sitting-together time for talking, reading picture books, and connecting.

> Teach calming techniques like deep breathing, snuggling with a blanket, and seeking help.

> Include stuffed animals, puppets, and baby doll activities to promote vicarious soothing. Accept that children may use construction or other play materials to reenact a stressful event. Offer words that seem to match what they are feeling as well as words of reassurance and comfort.

> Recognize that children "may need frequent, explicit, and consistent reminders that they are psychologically and physically safe" (NAEYC 2020a, 17). Be ready to seek mental health experts and other supports and resources that can assist you and families when they welcome this assistance.

Environments can also have negative impacts on children's development. There is extensive evidence showing that children who experience adverse circumstances, such as emotional and physical abuse, living with someone who suffers from depression or mental illness, or having an incarcerated family member, are negatively impacted (CDC 2023). These ACEs impact children's cognitive development as well as their social and emotional and physical development. ACEs have been found to increase children's risk of "sleep disturbance, failure to thrive, growth and developmental delays, viral and bacterial infection, atopic disease (including asthma, allergies, and eczema), overweight and obesity, and learning and behavioral difficulties" (NASEM 2019, 204–5). Racism must also be recognized "not only for its immediate and obvious impacts on children, but also for its long-term negative impacts, in which the repetitive trauma created by racism can predispose individuals to chronic disease" (NAEYC 2020a, 8). (See "Stress and Trauma, Including Racial Trauma, Affect Children's Learning.") In addition, the physical environment can greatly affect children's development. As just one example, as climate change continues to have impacts on all of us, children included, extreme heat can affect children's health and development, with effects felt throughout their lives (Early Childhood Scientific Council on Equity and the Environment 2023).

Stress and Trauma, Including Racial Trauma, Affect Children's Learning

When children experience losses and adverse circumstances, they grapple with a number of emotions and often don't have the cognitive capacity or language skills to process the events or articulate what they are experiencing. For example, Black children may continually witness someone who looks like them, their father, their mother, or other loved one be expelled, mistreated, or, in the worst case, killed. They are vulnerable to racial trauma (Jernigan & Daniel 2011; Saleem, Anderson, & Williams 2020) and may not be able to express their fear and distress in a way that's recognizable to some teachers. An Asian American child who witnesses someone telling their family to "go back where you came from" may begin acting aggressively toward their peers or withdrawing from participating in the classroom. While there is a need for more research on racism and its impact on children, children take in a great deal of information from their environments and begin to draw conclusions—yes, they are scientists in the making! There is evidence that children begin to see race as early as 3 months old; they gaze more at faces that look like their caregivers (Singarajah et al. 2017). As young as 3 years old, children begin to make decisions based on race, such as choosing preferred peers, with White children preferring to play with those who look like them and excluding those who don't look like them based on skin color and other factors (Derman-Sparks & Edwards, with Goins 2020; Iruka et al. 2020). Early childhood educators have always voiced a conviction that every child matters, regardless of race, ethnicity, gender, culture, religion, or creed. Unfortunately, the United States is built on systemic and structural racism that has permeated every institution and system through policies and practices that position people of color in oppressive, repressive, and menial positions. The early education system is not immune to these forces. In addition to the home and community environments, early learning settings are one of the central handful of places where children begin to see how they are represented in society. Thus, the early learning setting can be a place of affirmation and healing for children, or it can be a space of trauma, terror, and exclusion. Educators must work to ensure that it is the former.

The beauty of the brain, however, is its plasticity—the ability to compensate, regenerate, and develop different pathways to overcome the deleterious effects caused by traumatic experiences and adverse environments (Hunter, Gray, & McEwen 2018). Environment, as both a positive influence and a negative one, plays a significant role in children's development (National Scientific Council on the Developing Child 2023). It is the educator's role to create the type of environment that nurtures the health and development of every child.

IHEOMA U. IRUKA, PhD, is a professor of maternal child health in the Gillings School of Global Public Health, a fellow at the Frank Porter Graham (FPG) Child Development Institute, and the founding director of the Equity Research Action Coalition at FPG. Her work is focused on ensuring excellence for young diverse learners, especially Black children, and their families.

CHAPTER 4

The First Step for Addressing Bias in Infant and Toddler Programs

Sarah MacLaughlin

"Why are you still holding Prisha? She's asleep," Ms. Talia, an infant caregiver at a large child care center, asks her coworker, Ms. Janae.

"Because she likes being held and I like holding her," Ms. Janae replies.

· · · · · · · · · · · · ·

Three-year-old George arrives at school with his mother, Ms. Lei. "He wasn't hungry for breakfast earlier, so I'll just feed him here before I leave," Ms. Lei says to George's teacher. She sits in a small chair next to George and spoon-feeds him from a thermos of warm oatmeal.

· · · · · · · · · · · · ·

Braydon, 20 months old, wears a tutu while playing in the dramatic play area. His dad arrives to pick him up and asks, "Why are you wearing that?"

"I'm playing," Braydon replies.

"Take that off," responds his father. Braydon removes the tutu and hangs it on a low hook. His dad picks him up and walks out of the dramatic play area.

Before reading further, assess your reactions to these scenarios. Do you find yourself forming opinions? Do you relate closely to one of the teachers or parents in the scenarios? Does a mom spoon-feeding an older toddler make you pause or feel uncomfortable? Are you inclined to agree or disagree with the dad who reacted strongly to his son's dress-up choice?

These are situations that, when reflected on, help teachers identify their own beliefs and biases and those of others. Awareness of beliefs and biases is important for growing as an intentional teacher; both your gut reactions and your carefully considered opinions influence your behaviors, so the more you reflect, the

better prepared you can be to respond in supportive ways to situations that regularly present themselves in infant and toddler settings.

Many of the ways infant and toddler teachers think about and care for babies are quite personal and come from their own upbringings and cultures, at times eliciting strong feelings. How you hold, feed, and nurture comes in part from the ways you were treated as an infant and from the ideas your family and culture have about caring for young children. In each vignette that opens this chapter, the adults do what they genuinely think is best. But belief systems and our seemingly automatic reactions—on the surface so logical and rational—can both result from and fuel unintentional, internalized, and deeply held biases. In early childhood settings, a critical first step in addressing biases you may hold, and implementing an anti-bias approach in your program, is recognizing and being attuned to your internal beliefs and reactions. Self-awareness is vital in your work, as beliefs and biases influence not only how you care for children but also how you see the care that others provide.

Implementing an anti-bias approach in early childhood education facilitates a safe, nurturing, and inclusive learning environment (for more on the core goals of anti-bias education, see Derman-Sparks & Edwards 2019). All young children should have a sense of belonging so they are able to explore themselves, their families and communities, and their world in healthy, happy ways. Ideally, educators and children engaged in anti-bias education will develop awareness and appreciation of diversity—including age, race, ethnicity, culture, gender, sexual orientation, ability, belief system, and socioeconomic level—in their communities and beyond. As they learn to recognize unfairness, both children and adults can gain the skills and confidence to stand up for themselves and others against injustice (Derman-Sparks & Edwards, with Goins 2020).

Mitigating bias and creating inclusive curricula in early childhood settings are complex processes, involving much more than adding materials that highlight diversity to the classroom walls, toy shelves, and book collection. As Gonzalez-Mena notes,

> Adults working with infants and toddlers need to be vigilant about the verbal and nonverbal messages they convey. All children need outstanding models of adults who demonstrate effective and equitable interactions even in the face of conflict. Respectful care and thoughtful, loving relationships are the most powerful ways to give infants and toddlers an anti-bias, multicultural education. (2010, 151)

Opening Your Eyes and Heart

To "provide an inclusive educational environment where all children can succeed" (Derman-Sparks 1989, 40), teachers and caregivers must be open to the fact that they have their own hidden biases that need to be explored. The way to find biases is by paying attention to the small things that cause you discomfort or make you bristle. Following your discomfort can help you uncover these thoughts, many of which tend to be hidden under our good intentions.

Becoming and remaining mindful of biases and associations and the ways they spill over into judgments and prejudices is difficult. It requires ongoing, intentional effort. Awareness of your trigger moments—when you have a stronger-than-expected reaction to a person or practice—is a good indicator that there may be bias at work.

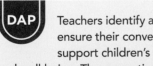 Teachers identify and reflect on bias to ensure their conversations and actions support children's positive development and well-being. These practices also help identify culturally and linguistically responsive learning experiences that will promote each child's identity.

Think About It

Consider these questions to probe a little deeper into possible biases you might hold.

- Have you ever had a strong reaction to an adult-child interaction you observed? If so, were you able to reflect on whether your reaction was grounded in bias? Sometimes it is. Teachers need to develop open-mindedness to allow all children to flourish and to appreciate that this flourishing happens in different ways.

- Have you ever noticed a bias you have toward someone because of their race, age, sexual orientation, gender, ethnicity, disability, style of dress, or other factor? Why do you think you have that bias? Has your awareness caused any changes in your behavior?

- How would you feel if a coworker pointed out a bias in your behavior? Would you feel initial discomfort? When confronted with a potential bias (whether from self-reflection or a colleague's observation), could you ask yourself, "Might it be true?" Could you be open to ways of addressing that bias?

Try It

Follow up your self-reflection with these action steps:

- Commit to reflecting on your feelings and actions regularly in an attempt to identify beliefs and biases.

- Do not become discouraged when you discover your biases. Noticing is the first step toward changing your beliefs and behaviors.

- Invite your colleagues to help you create a culture of noticing, questioning, and giving peer feedback at your workplace. Explore a variety of ways to do this collaboratively, such as peer mentoring, joint observations of one another's work, and brown bag lunch discussions focused on issues of culture and bias.

- When you experience discomfort with someone's behavior, acknowledge that feeling to yourself and reflect on the potential causes of your discomfort before reacting or responding (notice, wait, think, respond).

- Start an anti-bias task force at your school or center:

  - Be willing to experience discomfort. Aim for a work culture that embraces conflict resolution.

- Share and discuss books, articles, blogs, and other websites (see, e.g., NAEYC.org/resources/topics/anti-bias and www.teachingforchange.org/educator-resources/anti-bias-education).

- Plan authentic ways to engage families in sharing their diverse cultures—such as sharing stories, lullabies, feeding approaches, comforting techniques, playtime activities, and other meaningful routines.

Identifying and Addressing Bias in Observations and Interactions

by Marie Masterson

Conversations with families and children require sensitivity, objectivity, and fairness. Overcoming bias begins with self-inquiry and self-reflection, including exploring the ways bias can impact one's perceptions, interactions, judgments, and decisions. Melinda Miller (2022, 31) provides helpful definitions that can guide the journey of compassionate self-awareness and awareness of others. An intentional anti-bias mindset can help educators become intentional about monitoring their thought processes—and resulting actions—to ensure all families and children experience a sense of belonging, respect, and fairness.

> **Affinity bias** means "treating people more favorably, simply because of similarities such as skin color, appearance, education, or family structure."

> **Attribution bias** includes judging the experiences and accomplishments of others incorrectly, for example, attributing someone's success to "advantage or luck, as opposed to their effort, resilience, or skill."

> **Perception bias** means responding to people "based on simplistic assumptions and harmful stereotypes, as opposed to reality."

> **Confirmation bias** includes paying more attention or giving more weight to situations that confirm your beliefs or are based on your own "experiences, beliefs, or preconceptions."

The following action steps can help you identify and remove bias from observations and interactions with colleagues, families, and children:

> Meet with colleagues to share insights and learn from the perspectives of others to address and remove affinity, attribution, perception, and confirmation biases.

> Use strengths-based language with and about children and families during conversations with colleagues.

> Evaluate spoken and written messages to ensure these communicate appreciation and respect for the many diverse contexts of families and children.

> Reflect family contexts and cultures in classroom stories, music, conversations, materials, and activities.

> Include families as full partners by seeking their perspectives and insights as essential for goal setting and decision making.

Teachers of infants and toddlers have frequent opportunities to support young children in forming anti-bias attitudes. But these attitudes must first be modeled by teachers and caregivers themselves. An integral part of anti-bias work occurs when early childhood educators reflect on their personal worldview—hard-won insight that comes with greater awareness and a willingness to work together to effect change.

SARAH MacLAUGHLIN, LSW, is the senior training and technical assistance specialist for the Pediatrics Supporting Parents program at ZERO TO THREE and an award-winning author.

Engaging in Reciprocal Partnerships with Families and Fostering Community Connections

RECOMMENDATIONS FROM THE DAP STATEMENT

Developmentally appropriate practice requires deep knowledge about each child, including the context within which each child is living. Educators acquire much of this knowledge through respectful, reciprocal relationships with children's families. Across all ages, families' expertise about their own children is sought out and valued.

As you explore the components of developmentally appropriate practice and apply these to working with infants and toddlers, you may wonder how to incorporate principles of equitable and joyful learning at the earliest stages of development. How can you create a welcoming space where families from many social, cultural, and linguistic contexts experience a sense of purpose contributing to the life and vitality of the program? How can you remove barriers to trusting communication? How do you hold conversations about children's development in a way that honors families as children's first and most important teachers? It all begins with establishing a partnership with families, based on trust and respect.

> Eighteen-month-old Lilianna reaches from her teacher, Ms. Charlotte, to her mother, who arrives to pick her up. "I'm so happy to see you back," says Ms. Charlotte to Ms. Pérez. "Today, I sang 'Duerme Ya, Dulce Bien' (Sleep Now, Dear One) to Lilianna, and she slept soundly. Thank you for teaching me this lullaby and showing me how she likes to be held." "Oh, I'm happy," responds Ms. Pérez. "Lilianna is anxious because of the changes in our routine while I was visiting my mother. It's hard to be gone from the children, so I'm glad she is with you." Ms. Charlotte leans down to smile at Lilianna's brother, Luis, who is 4. "Mama said you read books and were a big helper while she was gone." Luis

smiles and hugs Ms. Charlotte. "Please have a good night," she says to the family. "I can't wait to see Lilianna again tomorrow."

Ms. Charlotte views this family as capable and strong. She frequently asks how things are going at home and what she can do to support Lilianna. She knows the names of extended family members and when Ms. Pérez is traveling. This authentic partnership instills trust and creates a cohesive and secure experience for Lilianna.

Educators look beyond their own understanding to seek knowledge and insight from families—one of their most important sources of information about the children they work with. Their goal is to engage with families through meaningful conversations and to develop understanding about linguistic and cultural contexts by observing the ways families care for and teach children. Educators also seek to learn about the neighborhood and community in which they work and explore the resources and services available to children and families. All of this work is foundational to understanding the ways infants and toddlers develop and learn in the context of their families and communities.

As families experience daily interaction with your program, they should notice warm and caring routines that are supportive of their children's comfort and learning and that are coordinated with their own. They see interactions that are personal and safe and that respect their own ways of caring for children. They appreciate when you make learning experiences personal for their children by choosing stories, songs, finger plays, activities, and other elements that reflect their own lives, contexts, and cultures. When a child has developmental delays or disabilities, the respectful relationship you are building with the family enables you to coordinate communication more smoothly between the family and specialists and to provide the family opportunities to contribute meaningfully to setting priorities and goals.

Working toward shared goals and offering many ways for families to participate in the program promotes trust and respect. When cultures or languages present a barrier to inclusion, using interpreters or volunteers identified by the family creates a safe and welcoming experience. Practicing self-reflection and engaging in dialogue with colleagues can help to ensure that your communication is strengths based and that barriers to engagement are removed. As a result, children benefit from shared decision making and goal setting and mutual celebration of their skills and achievements.

In Part 2, you will consider ways family engagement is the most important resource for infant and toddler teaching. You will read about family stories and educators' experiences of collaborating with families, with strategies and ideas to develop or enhance inclusive and meaningful partnerships with families.

READ AND REFLECT

As you read the chapters in this section, consider and evaluate your own classroom practices using these reflection questions.

"Creating Partnerships to Support Families of Infants and Toddlers" introduces developmentally appropriate family engagement practices through the lens of culture and continuity of care. It explores the perspectives of families and the need to provide emotional security, belonging, and acceptance for children. **Consider:** Think about the ways children make sense of themselves and create meaning from their experiences observing others. Do your communications with families and the decisions you make reflect strengths-based mindsets and language? What are some ways you connect with families to learn about the contexts and systems that impact children's lives?

"Engaging with Families to Individualize Teaching" shows the insight teachers gain as they learn from families' priorities and goals. It explores the often invisible dynamics that can influence communication and shows how teachers can incorporate family practices in programs. **Consider:** Why can expectations and norms related to caring routines and teaching remain hidden? How do you reserve judgment when family practices differ from your own? How can you use differences as opportunities to connect and build trust?

"Facilitating a Child's Transition from Home to Program Through the Use of Cultural Caring Routines" demonstrates the role of intentional teaching and the need to establish a trusting relationship with families as their child begins in the program. **Consider:** Why are

cultural and linguistic differences valuable resources for teachers when planning routines and interactions? What ways of being and interacting do families use that you can also use when interacting with children?

"Speaking Out: Supporting Families in Advocacy" presents a broad range of impacts teachers have when they advocate for children in the program, maximize support from specialists, bring together community services, and remove barriers to equity. **Consider:** What needs do your families have? If you don't know, how might you identify them? What resources are available in the community, and how can you connect families to these resources? What steps can you take to develop greater awareness of families' experiences and empower them in advocating for their children?

NEXT STEPS

After reading Part 2, consider the following suggestions as you plan next steps to foster your partnerships with families.

1. What successful strategies have you used to develop trusting relationships? List additional steps you would like to take to include families more consistently in conversations about children and in the program's activities.

2. What have you learned from families that has been most helpful to you in teaching? How can you share this information with other teachers who might benefit from your experiences?

3. Identify one or two barriers to family engagement you would like to overcome. What resources do you have to help you address these barriers? What other resources (including people) could you seek out? What is the first step you can take?

References for the chapters in this part can be accessed online at NAEYC.org/books/focus-infants-toddlers.

CHAPTER 5

Creating Partnerships to Support Families of Infants and Toddlers

Kelly Ramsey

Aisha is dropped off each morning at 6:00 a.m. when the center opens so her mom can get to work by 7:00 a.m. across town. Each week, Aisha is greeted by the same teacher who's held her in her arms since she was 6 weeks old. Now, at a year old, Aisha and the teacher have a relationship they can depend on daily. The consistent morning routine has established an understanding of what Aisha needs and how the teacher can partner with her.

This relationship started before the first day of school. The family sought a program that resonated with their culture and way of being. Their first visit to the program was held in a comfortable space to dialogue with teachers and see how the program embodies a welcoming learning community. In the initial meeting, the teacher shared how she honors families' caregiving routines and partners with families in making decisions about children.

Today, the drop-off routine for Aisha is seamless. The family and teacher have learned how to use a daily log and check-in notes to communicate about changes to the routine at home and school. As her mother leaves for work, Aisha hugs her goodbye and easily transitions to the classroom. The reciprocal relationship that has been built over the months between this teacher and child provides space for learning together. This is a picture of a reciprocal relationship fostering respectful teaching, family engagement, child-centered collaboration, and partnership.

As an educator working with children and families in a range of capacities over the years, I experienced and observed caregivers working in partnership to welcome infants and toddlers and their families to their programs. Throughout this work I noticed some key ways educators created partnerships with families as they parent their very young children, including

> Understanding families' cultures

> Understanding and supporting families on their journey as caregivers for their child, including sharing the meaning of children's behaviors as they grow and develop

> Creating a sense of belonging for families

> Reflecting on one's role and mindset as an educator

I have pulled from a wide range of range of theorists and resources as I have thought about how educators create strong partnerships with the families of infants and toddlers.

Understanding Families Through the Lens of Culture

Culture shapes the context for the social interactions that form the fundamental building blocks of the various dimensions of identity. It is through cultural learning that children gain a feeling of belonging, a sense of personal history, and security in knowing who they are. (Day 2013, 3)

Understanding families through the lens of culture and continuity of care is central to building enriched family engagement foundations. Putting families first—including acknowledging families' choices and goals for their child and responding with sensitivity and respect to those preferences and concerns—centers families from the beginning of the relationship. Care and learning practices that are culturally authentic and consistent with those in the home contribute to infants' and toddlers' development of sense of self (Day 2013).

The following concepts are key to gaining a better understanding of your families' cultures:

> Culture is a set of rules for behavior.

> Culture is characteristic of groups.

> Culture is learned.

> Individuals are embedded, to different degrees, within a culture.

> Cultures borrow and share rules.

> Members of a cultural group may be proficient in cultural behavior but unable to describe the rules. (Day 2013, 6)

As families enter a program, they are looking for a connection with the teachers. Caring for the child is the central focus for both the family and the program. Infant and toddler teachers partner with families to nurture the child and gain an understanding of family culture as a foundation to inform teaching decisions. To understand children, teachers ensure that families are listened to and experience respectful interactions with staff. These reciprocal relationships create lasting bonds and connections for the child, the teacher, and the family and enable teacher and family to make shared teaching decisions.

Tips for Understanding the Community of the Program and Families

Infant and toddler teachers' knowledge base should include understanding the communities they are working in and the families they serve. Many early childhood educators do not live in the same community in which the program is located and where the families live. If you are not familiar with the surrounding community, here are some ways you might get to know it and community members better:

> Visit a local grocery store to learn how families engage in the community.

> Take a drive around to see what the neighborhoods offer.

> Make a list of places like the park, libraries, and places to gather as a family.

> Ask families and other community members to share their personal experiences as participants in the life of the neighborhood and community.

> Explore the community history, including its development, industries, and contributions to its cultures over time. Search the internet, visit the local library, and/or talk to longtime community members.

Understanding and Supporting the Family's Journey Through Parenthood

Just as each child is on a developmental journey, teachers recognize that each family is also on a developmental journey through parenthood. Both journeys invite the building of partnerships. In the book *The Emotional Life of the Toddler*, Alicia Lieberman offers some understanding of how parents build partnerships with their toddler:

To help their child in this process of learning and discovering themselves, parents need to cultivate an attitude of partnership with the child, developing give and take between the child and the parent. This interaction is guided by the parent's awareness of the age-appropriate rights and responsibilities of the child. It is how a secure base for meaning making evolves into a partnership (Lieberman 1995, 32)

Meaning making, in this sense, refers to the parent's use of observations of their child's actions to understand what the child is saying or communicating. Teachers can support families' meaning making. For example, at drop-off a parent is holding the toddler in their arms, and the toddler is squirming and saying, "Down, down . . ." Seeing this, the teacher responds to the child's action and words by saying, "Oh, you said, 'Down.' You are ready to get down and walk by yourself?" This is an opportunity to use meaning making of the child's behaviors to connect with the family's journey with that child. This approach views the family as a collaborator with the child, similar to how teachers follow the lead of the child when partnering in their learning and discovery.

The family is navigating day-to-day situations to take care of each other and to nurture their young learner, just as the child is discovering the world around them. In the book *The Stages of Parenthood*, Ellen Galinsky (1987) provides a framework for understanding parental stages of development, identifying six stages: image making, nurturing, authority, interpretive, interdependent, and departure. A knowledge of what families experience and learn during the first couple of stages of raising their children can help infant and toddler teachers support families.

In stage one, parents are imagining what parenting will be like. Teachers, with their knowledge of children's developmental levels, can share with families their experiences to help families understand what to expect and how to navigate the growth and learning they may be observing in their children. In stage two, nurturing, parents can partner with teachers and the child. Galinsky describes the context in which the parenting relationship is designed in collaboration with the teacher. During this stage, the parent allows space to connect and create partnerships with teachers and others to support the child's growth and development.

As teachers engage with families to talk about caregiving routines and infants' and toddlers' experiences with the world around them, they have an opportunity to support developmental progress. Teachers can create an individualized notebook to share with families stories about their children's development while in the program, such as first steps, progress in walking, and language development from babbling to enunciation of sounds and words. The notebook can be passed back and forth between home and school so families can contribute as well. Together, teachers and families can use the notebook to plan individualized experiences for children based on what they might be ready to explore and learn next.

In their framework for understanding infants and toddlers, Mary Jane Maguire-Fong and Marsha Peralta (2018), authors of *Infant and Toddler Development from Conception to Age Three,* share what's going on with the parent and what's going on for the child as they are growing, moving, and developing. Teachers can draw attention to the ways a child communicates and makes choices and point out the ways the family follows the child's lead. This guided dialogue offers an opportunity for both the parent and teacher to learn about the child. Teachers can consider how the child interacts with their family members. What attention and focus does the child have? How is the child expressing whether they enjoy the interaction or experience? Are they smiling? Are they crawling away? What does the behavior mean? Families and teachers can share insights and ask clarifying questions to further understand what children are expressing.

Creating a Sense of Belonging for Families

Family engagement focuses on developing space— literal and figurative—to create a sense of place and honor families' contexts and strengths (Koralek, Nemeth, & Ramsey 2019). Including a space at the entryway of the program where families can gather, sit, and talk with other families and enjoy a book reading with their children communicates that families belong and that the program has made space and time for them. Adding child- and adult-sized furniture and plants in different areas creates additional welcoming spaces for children and families and is a good way to begin fostering a sense of belonging within the center community. You can also create space in program agendas for family voices and for teachers' sharing of practices, what they've learned with children, and how they've used family contributions to continue to foster engagement with children.

As you examine the context of how family engagement happens, consider what's in the environment in some settings, such as Early Head Start programs. Families are engaged throughout their enrollment process and are invited to be a part of the daily activities in the classroom and take on leadership roles on the parent council. What's created in these spaces is an open forum to have discussions, ask questions, foster a sense of belonging, and build a leadership pipeline for families.

Reflecting on Your Roles and Mindset

Context matters, for families and for educators too. Teachers and programs define what their work is, how they will go about that work, in what ways they are going to connect with families, and so on. As you consider the context for your work as an infant and toddler teacher, think about the roles you play. What questions can you consider as you talk with families and children that will help you get to know them and their goals and dreams? Here are just a few you might ask: What activities does the child take part in at home? What other family members or friends are important to the child's identity and relationships? What activities and experiences do these people enjoy with the child? What resources are part of the child's life outside of the program, such as a park or library? What activities in the community has the child and family attended? As families share their answers to these questions with you, you will develop a fuller understanding of the children's lives and identities outside of the program. You can use this information to create a welcoming, equitable, and joyful learning community for children and families.

All parents have important knowledge and perspectives to share about their children, and all have strengths that you can use as a framework for creating a new view of families. As you build a partnership with families, consider what deficit mindsets you might be holding about the children and their families, and how you can instead view them through a strengths-based lens. The Touchpoints Model of Development (Brazelton & Sparrow 2006) provides strategies to aid this process. One important strategy is to shift from the use of deficit language to language that is strengths based. The Touchpoints approach centers work with families and teachers on the periods during a child's first year when something changes in the child's development, requiring different responses from parents. This understanding creates a starting place for teachers to work in collaboration with families. The child brings the teacher and the family together so both can understand the child's strengths and talk about how to support learning and development. For example, the toddler squirming in his parent's arms mentioned previously is moving from wanting to be held to wanting to get down and explore on his own. By putting into words what the toddler appears to be communicating by this behavior—independence, eagerness to try out emerging skills—the teacher is assisting in meaning making and also signaling where the child is in their physical development.

Practical Strategies for Engaging Families of Infants and Toddlers

Here are 10 strategies to enhance family engagement in your program:

1. Create a welcoming space.

2. Spend time getting to know your families.

3. Create daily communication that respects and meets both the family's needs and your own.

4. Assign primary caregivers for routine caregiving that nurtures the child.

5. View infants and toddlers as capable learners.

6. Embrace the moments of wonder and discovery and share these regularly with families.

7. Invite families into the classroom to interact with their children and gain a sense of belonging in the learning space.

8. Share practical strategies you use in the classroom to bridge home and school. Ask families what their child is doing at home and about the strategies the family uses.

9. Build on strengths-based language and practices.

10. Provide equitable access to the classroom by engaging with families in meaningful cultural experiences and traditions.

Continuing to Build on Reciprocal Partnerships with Families

Reciprocal partnerships with families provide for an exchange. Teachers and families are learning from one another and listening—teachers are listening not to teach but to gain understanding (NAEYC 2022). Partnerships require a plan of action, including outlining how to implement strategies to create family engagement all year long and updating as needed.

Use simple strategies to initiate shared communication with families. To get started, begin with the end in mind. By creating a vision of what you want to see as an outcome, you have an aim to work toward. In addition to face-to-face communication and a daily notebook, you might communicate with families through text messages, phone calls, and/or video calls. It's important to develop and share action plans for caregiving routines, which can be captured on a daily sheet that records the child's sleep, feeding plans, and activities each day. Use electronic documentation methods or additional checklists that are shared between home and school. Take photos and create captions that document growth and learning. Families can also create documentation and add to the story by sharing the new discoveries and preferences they see at home. Consistently using communication tools that meet families' needs will support collaboration and enhance family-teacher partnerships.

Successful family engagement begins when teachers learn about families' experiences, understand the daily life of their child, and commit to ongoing, reciprocal, respectful communication. It requires a growing understanding of the family over time and supporting them as their child's first teachers. Through intentional and practical action steps, like reaching out in meaningful ways and nurturing authentic and caring relationships, you will foster family engagement that benefits everyone.

Additional Resources

These resources are centered on strengths-based practices:

> Brazelton Touchpoints Center. www.brazeltontouchpoints.org

> WestEd's Program for Infant/Toddler Care (PITC). www.wested.org/project/program-for -infant-toddler-care

> Janet Gonzalez-Mena, *Child, Family, and Community: Family-Centered Early Care and Education*, seventh edition. 2017.

> NAEYC Family Engagement Resources. NAEYC.org/resources/topics/family-engagement

> Zero to Three Child Development Resources. www.zerotothree.org/resources/

> CDC (Centers for Disease Control and Prevention) Milestones. www.cdc.gov/ncbddd/ actearly/milestones/index.html

> Early Head Start Programs. https://eclkc.ohs .acf.hhs.gov/programs/article/early-head -start-programs

KELLY RAMSEY has contributed to the field of early care and education for more than three decades as a classroom teacher, child care center director, training coordinator, national leader, college professor, and author.

CHAPTER 6

Engaging with Families to Individualize Teaching

Marie L. Masterson

What does it mean to engage with families? I like this description: "The difference between parent involvement and family engagement is the difference between 'doing to' and 'doing with.' As one teacher succinctly puts it, 'Instead of using your mouth to give instructions to families, you use your ears to listen'" (Ferlazzo 2012).

The concept of family engagement as a partnership or reciprocal relationship is well supported by the field and in particular by NAEYC, being embedded in NAEYC's position statement on DAP (2020a), early learning program standards (2018), professional standards and competencies for early childhood educators (2020b), and position statement on advancing equity (2019).

While dispositions like respect, kindness, and authentic caring are essential for educators, teachers need additional skills to build bridges with families when ideas differ or communication is unclear. "Doing with" families includes observing the ways they interact with children and actively listening to understand their perspectives and priorities. Educators must explore often complex dynamics that may otherwise remain as hidden barriers to collaboration. This chapter examines a scenario that reflects the emotional investment families feel and illustrates the ways teachers can become more sensitive learners and create positive solutions with families.

On the first day that 8-month-old Adella joins the classroom, Ms. Livy removes the infant's outer knit suit. Adella is wearing a beaded necklace and a bracelet. The bracelet, which has small beads woven through the red and black laces and a larger bead in the middle, leaves a red mark on Adella's arm. Adella has sucked on the bracelet, and it is damp from her saliva. Ms. Livy is concerned about cleanliness. She wonders if the beads present a choking hazard, but she doesn't say anything, not wanting to upset Ms. De Costa, Adella's mother.

Before leaving, Ms. De Costa places a small metal pot of homemade ointment into Ms. Livy's hands. She wants Ms. Livy to use it for diaper changes. Ms. Livy is unsure what to do, because the program has a written policy that all medications and ointments must be clearly labeled with the name of the child and a list of ingredients. She smiles and places the pot into the diaper bag. She plans to find out if this is allowable.

Ms. Livy wants to help Adella feel comfortable adjusting to the program. She also wants to honor the family's request and help Adella take pride in her family and culture. Ms. Livy and her director contact a cultural broker, a social worker from the community center, who understands the language and culture of the family and can share some ideas for incorporating the requests.

The cultural broker explains that in many cultures around the world, including Native American, Asian, and Latin American traditions, charms, beads, necklaces, bracelets, and anklets may be worn by infants for protection against disease or evil. In some religious traditions, jewelry is believed to provide protection from a guardian angel or saint and ward away evil spirits. Each bracelet or jewelry type may have a specific meaning to the family. Families believe this protection is essential for the safety of the child.

Ms. Livy and the director understand the importance of the jewelry to the family. In addition, they realize that making natural balms to aid in healing is part of Ms. De Costa's way of showing care for Adella. Ms. Livy talks with a licensing representative who works with programs to incorporate family requests. The representative says that the jewelry is okay since it is securely fastened. She also has a suggestion about how to incorporate the family's request to use the ointment. As a result, Ms. Livy asks Ms. De Costa for the list of ingredients. Ms. Livy records these on a card, adds Adella's name and the date, and places the card with the balm in a plastic bag.

The licensing representative shares some other family requests she is familiar with, such as touching infants while talking about them to avoid passing on negative energy, the use of gripe water (a liquid herbal supplement thought to soothe various infant ailments), and the preference for strict adult-determined sleep and feeding practices. She notes that many of these can be incorporated. However, she points out that when family practices are determined to be unsafe for children, additional consultation with the family will be necessary. For example, teachers must always place infants on their backs to sleep, and the crib may not contain clothing, restraints, or blankets that pose a strangulation risk. Nonnegotiable guidelines should be placed in the family handbook and discussed with families before children are enrolled. When licensing does not allow a practice, the director and teacher need to show sensitivity during conversations with the family.

The teachers come to know the De Costa family well and find caring ways to incorporate home practices into procedures and routines. While Ms. Livy and Ms. Sara, her coteacher, are not native Spanish speakers, they use the internet to find and learn frequently used words like *diaper, bottle, nap,* and *drink* in Spanish. They use the familiar names for the children's family members and use labels and captions to help them communicate. Over time, they continue to incorporate strategies to encourage Adella's development and learning.

One day Ms. Livy holds Adella on her lap. They sit on the soft carpet next to Ms. Sara, who is stacking cups with Gabe and Eva. The teachers have made personal photo books for each of the children. For the two infants from Spanish-speaking families, including Adella, the laminated books include captions in English with simple translations in Spanish.

Ms. Livy points to the colorful cover of Adella's book and says, "Where is Mamá? There's Mamá!" Adella smiles. "Is Mamá reading a book? You and Mamá like to read books together," says Ms. Livy as she turns the page. "Is this your dog? Es este tu perro?" Ms. Livy asks. She turns the page, covers up the photo of Adella with her hand, and asks, "Where is Adella?" She pulls her hand away and says, "There's Adella!" Adella laughs and claps her hands.

While changing Adella's diaper, Ms. Livy uses a picture guide above the changing table that shows a baby with each part of the body labeled in English and Spanish. Ms. Livy holds Adella's feet gently and says, "These are your feet. Esta son tus pies. And here are your toes. Dedos de los pies." Then she tickles Adella's fingers and says, "Tus dedos—your fingers." Ms. Livy uses ointment and slips on a clean diaper before replacing Adella's clothing. "All done, Adella! You are warm and dry," she says.

Ms. Livy spends time with Ms. De Costa to learn how Adella is rocked and fed. At first, Ms. Livy forgets, and she holds Adella facing toward her to take the bottle. She turns Adella around to rock against her shoulder, but Adella fusses and pushes away. Ms. Livy remembers that Ms. De Costa faced Adella outward, where she could watch Ms. Sara and the others. Ms. Livy adjusts Adella outward and tries to read *Tengo diez deditos* (*Ten Little Fingers*), but Adella doesn't seem interested.

Ms. Livy asks Ms. Sara to play a recording of "Duérmete Mi Niño" ("Fall Asleep My Child"). It was recorded by Ms. De Costa. Within a few minutes, Adella is asleep. Once she is placed in the crib, Ms. Livy plays soft music from *Canciones De Cuna: Spanish Lullabies*. These are songs that are soothing and familiar to Adella. The other children are going sleep and enjoy the melodies too.

As the teachers learn more about the families, they build trust as they honor the priorities that are valued. They continue to ask the families to demonstrate ways of playing and supporting the children. They gain deeper understanding about the families' practices and the children's unique ways of developing to help them make effective teaching decisions.

 Developing understanding of child development in context allows teachers to individualize their responses to each child. Consider the commonalities children share, and also identify unique traits, values, and ways of responding that are unique to each family.

Family Engagement Principles and Practices

Adapted from Sarah Erdman & Laura Colker, with Elizabeth Winter (2020)

Important principles lay the groundwork for a successful partnership between families and educators. First, teachers must take the lead to ensure communication is two-way and reciprocal. Second, they use a strengths-based approach that builds on family members' talents, skills, and interests. Finally, they seek to individualize interactions with each family.

Building on these principles, specific strategies for family engagement will help you develop positive relationships with families and also benefit children:

> Work with family members to jointly set goals and make decisions about their child. Challenges are best solved when families team with teachers. Sometimes teachers aren't aware of problems family members observe at home.

> Support children through transitions in their lives. Children need support from all sides when facing life's changes and challenges.

> Promote family well-being. Educators should constantly look for ways to best support children and families.

> Facilitate positive family-child relationships. Part of teaching is helping family members be the best they can be.

> Provide activities that can be done at home to support program learning. Children learn best when routines and activities they do at their program are reinforced at home.

> Connect families with other families in the program for social support and networking. Teachers can build parents' confidence, skills, and enjoyment by teaming them with fellow parents who share similar concerns and interests.

> Connect families to community support organizations and staff. Teachers are in a position to offer much-needed services to family members by maintaining current contact information for individuals and agencies that provide services to families with young children.

> Support families as lifelong educators of their children.

> Support families in their own educational needs and aspirations. Teachers have a professional obligation to help families—not just their children—thrive and flourish.

> Support families as child advocates. Advocacy enriches children, families, and the entire community.

Remember that culture—both a family's and your own—influences how a child's family will react to you both as an educator and as an individual and to the process of family engagement. Some families regard their child's educator as an expert to be granted deference and respect, some will be wary of your intentions and may view you as an intruder in their lives, some will challenge your knowledge and ideas, some will react hesitantly or even negatively in response to some aspect of your own culture, and others will welcome your invitations to be equal partners in their children's education.

Culture also influences family members' feelings about how the program should operate and what constitutes appropriate interactions between children and educators. If you find that a family's perspective differs from yours or your program's, your professional responsibility is to keep an open mind. Resist the temptation to jump in and "set the record straight." Listen to everyone's perspective and consider why they think this way. Often, viewpoints are not as far apart as they seem initially. Adjustments can be made so that everyone feels heard and respected. Cross-cultural communication requires critical listening, reflection, support, and practice.

Building Trust for Holding Difficult Conversations

How can educators overcome barriers to ensure families feel like equal partners rather than merely recipients of information or defensive? When conversations involve children's progress, adjustment, development, disabilities, or cultural differences, teachers should take the lead to build trust and help families feel safe to share their ideas and questions. The following strategies help to establish trust and promote collaboration:

> Affirm family insights and contributions as foundational to decision making.

> Ask questions such as "What do you find works best at home?" and "What else would you like me to know?"

> Identify strengths-based goals: "This is a great opportunity for us to encourage your child's strengths and use them as a bridge to help her develop new skills."

> Encourage families to discuss developmental issues with their family pediatrician or a specialist.

> Request support from professionals, experts, and cultural brokers to obtain additional insights.

> Seek online and community resources to help you and the children's families learn together.

MARIE MASTERSON, PhD, is an early childhood specialist, licensed teacher, and quality improvement consultant and trainer. She is director of quality assessment for the state of Illinois ExceleRate at McCormick Center for Early Childhood Leadership at National Louis University.

CHAPTER 7

Facilitating a Child's Transition from Home to Program Through the Use of Cultural Caring Routines

Josephine Ahmadein

Early childhood educators play a crucial role in the development and learning of very young children from culturally and linguistically diverse backgrounds. This chapter relates the story of how Ms. Jackie, a teacher of infants and toddlers, relies on understanding and adopting a family's cultural caring routines to provide a safe, smooth transition from home to group care for Pooja, a 10-month-old girl. The story illustrates how the critical connections between the adults involved in a child's life help to create a unique learning context that is essential for the child's successful development and learning. This teacher not only understands that there must be a coexistence between commonality and context (two core considerations of developmentally appropriate practice) to facilitate the growth and well-being of the infants in her care but also shows her understanding of the third core consideration, individuality, as she provides experiences based on each child's unique characteristics and experiences.

DAP Early childhood educators seek out and gain knowledge and understanding using three core considerations: commonality in children's development and learning, individuality reflecting each child's unique characteristics and experiences, and the context in which development and learning occur. These apply to all aspects of decision making to foster each child's optimal development and learning.

Two weeks before Pooja starts her first day in an infant-toddler classroom, Ms. Jackie contacts Pooja's parents, Mr. and Mrs. Gupta, to schedule an introductory meeting with them. Ms. Jackie wants to learn as much as she can about Pooja and her family, but she is also respectful of what Mr. and Mrs. Gupta are comfortable sharing regarding their cultural background, home language, Pooja's daily routines, and other important facts about Pooja. Ms. Jackie learns that Pooja has been taken care of at home since she was born and has not spent time with anyone outside the home. Even though Pooja's parents speak English with Ms. Jackie, they speak only Bengali, their home language, to Pooja. Ms. Jackie also learns that being held as much as possible is an essential part of her daily routine. Pooja only drinks liquefied foods fed to her in a bottle, almost always while being held by her mother. She has never been offered solid food, nor has she been introduced to a spoon.

Knowing Pooja has only heard Bengali, Ms. Jackie asks Pooja's parents to provide a list of words and short phrases in Bengali that she can use in the classroom to help Pooja adjust to her new environment. Mr. and Mrs. Gupta quickly agree to the suggestion and include on the list one of Pooja's favorite games, "Tai, tai, tai" (which means clap, clap, clap), as well as some of her favorite songs.

The Development of Trusting Relationships

As Mrs. Gupta is dropping off Pooja on the first day, Pooja emits loud, piercing cries and arches her back in protest. Though this makes it hard for Ms. Jackie to offer Mrs. Gupta reassuring words, she endeavors to do so in a positive, calm tone amid Pooja's inconsolable sadness "It's going to be okay, Mrs. Gupta. I will call you in a couple of hours to give you an update on Pooja." Ms. Jackie says. As Ms. Jackie comforts Pooja, she starts singing a fragment of a reassurance separation song that will become a daily, consistent element in forming the crucial trust that Pooja needs to thrive in her new environment:

> . . . 'cause my mommy comes back, she always comes back,
>
> Mommy comes back to get me. My mommy comes back,
>
> She always comes back.
>
> She never will forget me.

As the day goes on, Pooja occasionally looks around curiously at the children and toys around her, but she frequently cries and tries to pull away from Ms. Jackie to go toward the entrance door, where she last saw her mother. Ms. Jackie calmly acknowledges Pooja's emotions with familiar, reassuring words and songs.

During feeding time, sitting next to other infants in highchairs, Ms. Jackie holds Pooja on her lap and offers Pooja her bottle from home. She recalls the words and routines Pooja's mother shared with her during their introduction meeting and starts using them, like singing Pooja's favorite songs: "Twinkle, Twinkle, Little Star," "Snowflakes, Snowflakes," and "The Wheels on the Bus."

Ms. Jackie says, "Let's do some tai, tai, tai," as she claps her hands in one of Pooja's favorite games to keep Pooja motivated to keep feeding. This game elicits some happy laughter before Pooja yawns. Ms. Jackie says, "Ghumu korbe!" (Time to sleep!) and prepares Pooja for her nap.

Each day, Ms. Jackie remains patient and empathetic with Pooja. Slowly but consistently, Pooja makes progress. Ms. Jackie continues to invest time and thought in helping Pooja adjust to the program. She understands and practices what Chen and Ahmadein (2018) describe: "By incorporating the native cultures and languages of infants and toddlers into their authentic daily routines and activities, the caregivers naturally help to create necessary continuity and familiarity between the home and the childcare setting" (9).

For three weeks, Ms. Jackie feeds Pooja on her lap alongside the other infants who are sitting in highchairs. Then, one day, Pooja points to a chair next to other infants. No longer is she pushing back and turning her head forcefully around to avoid the spoon as she had done before.

Ms. Jackie asks, "Do you want to sit next to Jake and Ali?" Pooja smiles and lunges toward the highchair. Ms. Jackie happily sits Pooja down. Pooja begins to accept some table food too, though not yet from a spoon. She still prefers the food to be given to her by hand into her mouth. Watching Pooja eat her food, Ms. Jackie exclaims, "Umm, so good!"

Ms. Jackie shares Pooja's progress with Mrs. Gupta, who is very pleased to hear about it. However, at home, Mrs. Gupta continues to feed Pooja liquefied foods in her bottle whenever Pooja refuses solid foods. Ms. Jackie is concerned that in doing so, Pooja might take longer to accept finger foods and self-feed, both at home and at school. However, she continues to remain patient as she monitors Pooja's all-around progress and updates Mr. and Mrs. Gupta accordingly, gathering further data in case it is needed for future discussions.

While continuing to concentrate on consistent routines, Ms. Jackie has also started using sign language during the daily sing-alongs. She does the same during reading time. Imitating Ms. Jackie, Pooja begins to use some signs while singing along. Signing gradually becomes an additional tool of comfort and attachment for Pooja. Ms. Jackie suggests that Mr. and Mrs. Gupta use sign language with Pooja at home to facilitate the continuity of practice, and they both gladly accept this suggestion. Ms. Jackie also suggests letting Pooja hold her own spoon during solid feedings and singing her favorite songs to encourage Pooja to try table foods more.

 DAP Keeping track of changes in children's daily patterns and responses to routines provides important information to evaluate and share with families. Families respond to these details by offering practical insights and ideas for teaching decisions.

After three months, Ms. Jackie's hard work has paid off as she witnesses Pooja's physical, social, and emotional growth. For example, Pooja smiles and lunges forward to Ms. Jackie at drop-off times. Pooja has also learned to use her hands to hold food. Ms. Jackie has gained the trust of not only Pooja but also her parents. Her intentional efforts to form a positive partnership with Pooja's parents around Pooja's daily care and learning demonstrates her commitment "to engage them in a collaborative endeavor to promote their child's language development and multicultural learning" (Chen & Ahmadein 2018, 8). Importantly, Pooja's many positive interactions with Ms. Jackie have helped foster a growing secure attachment between infant and teacher.

Conclusion

Pooja and Ms. Jackie's story reinforces the importance of the continuity of learning between home and early childhood settings as well as a strong family-teacher partnership that benefits a child's development and learning. It highlights Ms. Jackie's intentional efforts to incorporate cultural and linguistic values and behaviors that are different from her own, thus demonstrating that she stands committed to "recognizing differences as variations in strength, not deficits" (Bredekamp & Willer 2022, 12). She demonstrates the value of embracing the whole child, including the home language and culture as strengths, and intentionally incorporates them in daily interactions with children.

Ms. Jackie relies on understanding and adopting the family's cultural caring routines to provide a safe, smooth transition from Pooja's home to the infant and toddler room. While Pooja makes progress as she adjusts to new routines, Ms. Jackie realizes that the work continues. She intentionally plans to continue introducing new words in English while integrating words that Pooja already knows in her home language. Her efforts will result in a continuous, comprehensive, and responsive learning experience for the child.

JOSEPHINE AHMADEIN, BA, IMH-E, is an early childhood quality improvement specialist (QIS) at Community Coordinated Child Care (CCCC) of Union County, New Jersey, infusing her more than 30 years of classroom experience with infants and toddlers into her work with educators and families.

CHAPTER 8

Speaking Out
Supporting Families in Advocacy

Kristen Johnson and Amanda Perez

Ms. Lorena recently started a new position in the toddler room at her child care center. Right away, she notices that Mauricio, 22 months old, is a born comedian. Last week, for example, he accidentally walked into the room's soft chair. When a few of his classmates laughed, Mauricio repeated the action again and again until those children—and a few more, and then Ms. Lorena—were all laughing.

But today, when his mother, Joanna, brings him in, she seems worried. This past weekend, Mauricio's 18-month-old cousin was in town. Joanna watched her nephew playing with Mauricio's blocks and stacking them high. She watched him at dinner and noticed how easily he fed himself. "Mauricio never slows down to play with blocks," she says, "and meals are so messy!"

Ms. Lorena does not yet know Mauricio well, but she nods as Joanna talks. "I am just learning about Mauricio," she says. "You have so much to teach me! If you have concerns, there are some local programs I can connect you with. If you'd like, we can talk you through the steps involved in reaching out."

Ms. Lorena is new to her setting, but she is building an important relationship with both Mauricio and his family. She knows that Joanna is her child's first teacher and lifelong advocate. She also knows that as Mauricio's early childhood educator, she has an opportunity to support both him and his family in building skills they will use for the rest of their lives. These include advocacy. As Ms. Lorena partners with Joanna in advocating for her child—both in the classroom and the community—Joanna gains the confidence and skills necessary to effectively articulate the needs, desires, and wishes that she has for Mauricio (Baba et al. 2016). This outreach also strengthens Ms. Lorena's knowledge and practices related to responsive family collaborations and her own advocacy efforts.

In its simplest definition, advocacy means "speaking out." Early childhood educators have the familiarity, expertise, and skills that make them key advocates for the children, families, programs, and communities they serve. Teachers also have an ethical responsibility to advocate for the children in their care (NAEYC 2011), and advocating for young children and their families is one of the ways educators demonstrate their professionalism (NAEYC 2020b).

Educators can empower families to become effective advocates too. Over a child's life, families will need to speak out for them in a variety of ways. These include:

> Talking with health care providers to address physical and/or mental health needs

> Meeting with educators, administrators, and/or specialists about supports children may need in the classroom

> Advocating for services or programs to help children grow and thrive

> Speaking up to ensure communities are safe, healthy, and equitable

As Ms. Lorena works with Joanna to access a developmental screening for Mauricio, she is assisting Joanna in her beginning advocacy efforts. This will benefit Mauricio and his family as he moves through preschool and beyond (National Center on Parent, Family, and Community Engagement, n.d.).

 EQUITY Supporting and giving voice to diverse perspectives strengthens the network of resources available to all children and families. Teachers establish collaborative relationships and ensure equitable access to social service agencies and community resources that strengthen families.

Strategies for Supporting Families in Advocacy

Parenting a baby, especially a first child, can be overwhelming. By helping Joanna recognize why and how her knowledge, beliefs, and experiences as a parent matter, Ms. Lorena provides an important mirror for Joanna that reflects back the image of an articulate and powerful advocate. This type of relationship can help families see themselves as competent and as experts about their children and their lived experiences. It also offers a sense of support and safety in conversations about children (Henderson, Kressley, & Frankel 2016).

Teachers of infants and toddlers can use several strategies to encourage and help develop their families' advocacy skills. A discussion of each follows.

Honor Family Expertise

Families play the primary role in their children's development and learning. As such, educators should look for a variety of ways to learn about and from their knowledge and experiences (NAEYC 2019, 2020a). These can include the following:

> Collecting information about family expertise and interests through enrollment forms, informal discussions, family conferences, and parent council meetings

> Asking families what they need or want for their children and suggesting resources or programs that can help

> Using a family's goals for their child as a source of information when planning the classroom curriculum and providing individualized, responsive care to each child

Through these efforts, families learn that their expertise can make a difference for their child—a realization that is often the first step to advocacy.

For example, as Ms. Lorena works with Joanna to access early intervention services, Joanna learns about available community resources that can answer her questions and potentially assist her child. She also learns that her knowledge of Mauricio both matters and spurs her son's teacher to action. This realization enhances Joanna's sense of competence and confidence as an advocate over time.

Listen to Families' Concerns

A teacher's day is busy, but it is important to prioritize family partnerships. Research shows that when educators encourage families to engage with them and the program (e.g., by inviting them to volunteer and attend meetings or by sharing what their child is doing in the classroom and showing interest in what the family sees their child doing at home), families are more likely to participate in the program by spending time in the classroom (Barnett et al. 2020). This gives families a closer look at routines, materials, and learning experiences in the classroom. Benefits abound for the educator and program too. They gain vital information about a child and family, which can inform decision making and practices.

Listen to the information families share about their children and take note of any underlying emotions or observations. Families may find it easier to show they are excited or worried about something that is happening than to describe what they're feeling. Then restate their concern and suggest action; for example: "It sounds like your child care subsidies are being cut, and you aren't sure why. That sounds really aggravating. There is a community meeting on child care coming up. Would you be interested in attending?" Keep a notepad near the classroom entrance to write down next steps that arise from conversations with families.

Keep Abreast of Available Resources

Families report that they trust early childhood educators and look to them for information about child development and community resources (Zero to Three 2018). When educators connect families with services, those families get a sense of the range of programs, resources, and systems in the community. This information can eventually inform further advocacy work. For example, early intervention is publicly funded and regulated. As Joanna gets involved with this system, she can use her experiences with Mauricio to help others in her community access programs or to push for funding or legislation at the policy level.

Advance Equity

In some ways, the concepts and approaches used by programs for family engagement and advocacy may be rooted in a primarily White, English-speaking, educationally and economically privileged mindset (Borgh et al. 2022). Educators should be willing to challenge these mindsets. For example, disagreeing with educators and administrators can feel incredibly disrespectful to families from many communities, so teachers might consider how advocacy can take place in ways that do not pit family opinions against educators'. One avenue is to gather information from families in a way that lets families offer their thoughts and opinions about their children and the program before educators or administrators offer their ideas.

Examining programs and seeking information from families about their social and cultural beliefs and practices can help in this effort to advance equity (NAEYC 2019). Questions to ask yourself, colleagues, and leaders include these:

> What do ideas like advocacy and leadership look like for the families a program serves?

> What are the pressing issues, concerns, or topics for families in the program?

> In what ways are families engaging in advocacy already? Are families comfortable advocating in ways that educators suggest, or are they looking for other ways to share their thoughts?

> What beliefs and assumptions guide the strategies and approaches a program uses to nurture advocacy? Are those beliefs and assumptions grounded in or biased toward White, English-speaking, educationally and/ or economically privileged experiences and perspectives?

> Are there particular groups who are left out of or underrepresented in advocacy efforts?

Seeking answers to these questions and acting on the insights gained will help center equity in advocacy efforts—both in the early learning program and the community.

Strategies to Expand Advocacy Efforts

Partnering with families to advocate for their children's growth and development is essential. Policy advocacy is slightly different but also critical. It means speaking out to support (or oppose) specific policies being considered or enacted within the broader local or national community. Often, when early childhood educators are called to do policy advocacy, families can offer valuable insights by sharing stories that illustrate the impact or promise of proposed actions for infants, toddlers, families, educators, and programs. Joining diverse perspectives and voices can lead to a far more powerful impact than one voice alone.

One caveat: Some early childhood settings may have policies and procedures in place that restrict the ways teachers can talk with families about policy advocacy. For example, public funding may prohibit particular kinds of policy conversations. Talk with your program's leadership to identify if—and how—local, state, and national advocacy opportunities can be shared with enrolled families.

Joanna's ability to share her concerns and questions about Mauricio's development gives Joanna the confidence to begin broadening her voice. For example, in conversations with other families, Joanna learns they have some common questions about parenting and child development. While staff is responsive to these questions, Joanna looks for additional resources. She begins advocating for a family library at the center. She solicits donations, then manages the checkout process once the library is opened.

When Ms. Lorena mentions that many early childhood educators are tempted by openings and better pay offered at the local elementary school, Joanna begins to advocate for higher wages for the teachers at her center. Building on her experiences, she talks with the director to learn more about the center's budget and staffing issues. She talks with other families to generate enthusiasm for action. She then partners with Ms. Lorena and the center's director to bring a group of staff and families to the state capitol to talk with policymakers about increasing investments in child care.

With Ms. Lorena's support and encouragement, Joanna has learned that her voice matters—for her son and so many others.

Think About It

Consider these questions to help you think more deeply about ways to advocate for families and support their own advocacy efforts:

> Consider how you encourage families to speak out. How do you gather or recognize their expertise about their children? How do you use the information they share? Can you support their advocacy efforts during your everyday interactions?

> Think about a success story: When did you connect with a family in a way that supported their advocacy?

> How familiar are you with the network of services your community offers young children? How well are you connecting families to these services?

> What are some critical policy issues facing your community right now? In what ways could the families in your program advocate for these issues? What can you do to nurture their efforts?

Try It

Follow up your reflection with these action steps:

> Consider all you know about the children in your setting (favorite toys, developmental milestones, social and cultural contexts, and more). Then consider what their families know that you might not (changes in family structure, nighttime routines, their children's relationships with family members and others outside the family, upcoming events). Brainstorm ways to build and expand your understanding of each family's context. Identify the regular times you connect with families. How do you use those times to learn about children and build a family's sense of expertise? Be intentional in the ways you nurture each family's confidence and sense of themselves as experts and advocates.

> Work with others on your staff to reflect on your program's family partnership strategies and leadership opportunities. Do you notice any biases or gaps, including those related to race and culture? Look at data related to how these strategies are being used and if they are effective for each and every family in your program. How can you bring more families into the conversation?

> Learn about the early childhood resources in your community, particularly how families can connect to child care subsidies, nutrition services, health services, and early intervention services.

> Learn more about how families are advocating for early education and care. Visit www.thinkbabies .org/policy-priorities-child-care for examples. How might these messages inform your own advocacy efforts?

When educators partner with families to best nurture young children, early education programs become learning environments for more than just the children. And with the skills and expertise they build together, educators and families become better able to educate other community members and even policymakers to make services and policies better supports for young children.

KRISTEN JOHNSON, MEd, is the executive director at-large at the Goddard Schools in metropolitan Atlanta and a member of the executive board of the Georgia Association for the Education of Young Children.

AMANDA PEREZ, MSW, serves as the senior advocacy manager at Zero to Three's Policy Center. She has worked with babies and families in child care, early intervention, Early Head Start, and advocacy.

PART 3

Observing, Documenting, and Assessing Children's Development and Learning

RECOMMENDATIONS FROM THE DAP STATEMENT

Observation, documentation, and assessment of young children's progress and achievements is ongoing, strategic, reflective, and purposeful. Educators embed assessment-related activities in the curriculum and in daily routines to facilitate authentic assessment and to make assessment an integral part of professional practice. The methods of assessment are responsive to the current developmental accomplishments, language(s), and experiences of young children. They recognize individual variation in learners and allow children to demonstrate their competencies in different ways.

Ms. Ashley sits next to 11-month-old Samuel on the floor and watches him roll side to side, holding his feet in his hands. He pushes over to his stomach and propels himself forward with a belly crawl, scooting with both back feet at once. She smiles and says, "Get the ball. Can you catch it?" Samuel reaches the ball successfully, presses into a sitting position, and grins. "Ba!" he says. Although the other children have been crawling for several months and most are cruising or walking, Samuel has demonstrated his own creative ways of moving. Ms. Ashley has been tracking his physical progress. Today, she has captured this sequence of movement on a digital video recording to show Samuel's family how well he is getting around the play spaces. She also writes a brief description of Samuel's morning play choices, noticing that he has eagerly joined the other children to drop animals and balls down the slide. She notes that the activity allows Samuel space and time to make choices independently while still enjoying the antics and laughter of the others. Ms. Ashley will use these notes to keep Samuel's family up to date as they collaborate to support his development.

Assessment, observation, and documentation of children's learning are essential ingredients of developmentally appropriate practice that are most effective when woven seamlessly into the daily life of routines and play. These practices work together to provide important information about children's progress. By using them in a variety of situations and at various times of day, educators gain a full picture of children's emerging skills, their strengths, and areas that need support.

You can capture children's advancing skills through a variety of documentation methods, including written notes, photos, recordings, and artwork. Portfolios allow you to share tangible and accurate examples and stories with families. As you reflect on children's skills and growth captured through your observations, you can apply the insights you gain to curriculum planning.

Involving families in interpreting assessment information and making shared decisions about the results is a vital part of the assessment process. Invite family members to regularly discuss children's experiences in the program and at home. Share even subtle aspects of social, emotional, and cognitive development, such as how children manage frustration or persist in reaching a goal. Celebrate children's milestones, and consider what areas need additional support.

Child screenings are designed to identify children who may need additional evaluation or support. In addition, screening tools are used to evaluate language, physical, and social and emotional development. Family members along with therapists, consultants, and the family's pediatrician contribute information essential for making decisions about early intervention services and planning for inclusive teaching.

As part of authentic and accurate evaluation, it is important to actively work against implicit and explicit bias. Methods of assessment should be used by educators and specialists who understand the culture and language of the child and family. Ensure that your observations, evaluations, and written and spoken messages are strengths based, expressing confidence in and understanding of each child's capabilities and assets. Understand the interdependence of developmental areas, the uneven nature of development in infants and toddlers, and day-to-day variations—and then use the results of observation, documentation, and assessment to design learning experiences that support emerging skills and build children's confidence during each step forward.

In Part 3, you will read about a range of developmentally appropriate strategies to enhance your observation, documentation, and assessment approaches with infants and toddlers.

READ AND REFLECT

As you read the chapters in this section, consider and evaluate your own classroom practices using these reflection questions.

"Bringing Observation and Documentation to Life in Infant and Toddler Settings" explores the way teachers learn about children's interests, developmental progress, and temperaments. When there are variations in children's behavior, these are recorded and used to reflect with colleagues, communicate with families, and plan teaching. Teachers adjust their approach to support children's strengths and skills. **Consider:** How do you use the information you gain from observing and assessing individual children to do the following: Make teaching decisions? Adjust your planning and teaching? Evaluate the effectiveness of your teaching strategies?

"Observation and Documentation: Both Art and Science" shows how teachers use observation as the starting point to activate inquiry-based learning, focusing on the ways children play, explore, and engage with their settings. This purposeful design becomes action research where teachers foster creativity, sensory learning, social skills, and cognitive development. **Consider:** How do observation and documentation make children's learning visible to families and others? What systems do you have in place to document changes in children's learning and development? How can documentation support you in responding to children?

"Using a Child-Centered Approach to Shift from a Deficit Mindset" illustrates how teachers work with specialists and families to provide individualized, responsive support for children with diverse characteristics, abilities, and needs. By using observation, reflection, and individualized teaching, teachers create inclusive and joyful learning experiences for all children. **Consider:** How can you build families' trust through reciprocal communication? How can you identify children's strengths and incorporate activities that offer multimodal engagement? What changes do you need to make to create a more inclusive classroom?

"Empowering Infants' and Toddlers' Learning Through Scaffolding" shows the practical and collaborative way observation and responsive scaffolding enrich learning for infants and toddlers. The authors provide a theoretical and research-based foundation for the benefits of scaffolding, with strategies to apply to planning, teaching, and interactions. **Consider:** Think about and observe the play your infants and toddlers are engaging in. How do they take the lead, and when do you take the lead? When do you step back and let them figure things out, and when do you assist?

"What Babies Ask of Us: Contexts to Support Learning About Self and Others" explores ways of teaching that promote sensitivity and attunement to infants and toddlers and their families. You will find strategies for reflective planning for play spaces, daily routines, and interactions. **Consider:** How can you use a cycle of reflective planning to follow children's current enjoyment and interests? Are you thoughtfully monitoring your own interactions to honor children's timing and choices and following their cues to encourage increasing independence and creativity? What can you change in your play spaces, routines, and conversations to better engage the children?

NEXT STEPS

After reading Part 3, consider the following suggestions as you plan next steps in your observation, documentation, and assessment processes.

1. Make a list of observation, documentation, and assessment strategies that work together to provide a comprehensive understanding of each child. What sources will you use to gather information to ensure an accurate picture of development and learning?

2. How will you practice self-refection and shared reflection to ensure that the information you capture and the messages you convey about children and their families are bias free and strengths based?

3. How can families more fully participate in the process of screening, referral, and resources sharing? How can you improve the ways you share documentation with families to make sure they feel fully included as collaborators and decision makers?

References for the chapters in this part can be accessed online at NAEYC.org/books/focus-infants-toddlers.

CHAPTER 9

Bringing Observation and Documentation to Life in Infant and Toddler Settings

Rebecca Parlakian

Gabriella, a teacher of 2- and 3-year-olds, looks over her class list. One of her children, Harrison, is absent again today. "Hmmm," she thinks. "Nine absences this month. I hope everything's all right." She makes a note to share the attendance information with her program's family support specialist; perhaps there's a way to support Harrison's family in their efforts to get him to school.

Next, Gabriella reaches into her pocket and pulls out several sticky notes. One says "Camila, cows, vocab." She remembers how earlier in the day, Camila had pulled the cow puppet onto her hand and told a story about the cow taking a bath. "Camila's vocabulary is really taking off," Gabriella thinks. "Maybe we could read some stories about farm animals if she's interested in cows. Or maybe we could do some water play and give all the toy animals a bath?"

A quick look at the calendar reminds Gabriella that at their next meeting, staff will hear about the results from a recent program-wide observation of teacher-child interactions and classroom climate. "I wonder what that will mean for our classroom," she thinks.

The experiences children have in early childhood influence their development and later school success. High-quality early education experiences provide a strong foundation that children build on for years to come. Specifically, children who experience higher quality care in early childhood settings are more likely to have better educational and social outcomes than children in lower quality settings development (Bustamante et al. 2021). These associations can persist into young adulthood, shining a spotlight on the central role that early learning experiences play in children's lives.

To help ensure a high-quality education, teachers of infants and toddlers can use meaningful assessment practices to guide their selection of curriculum and instructional approaches. These practices can also help you in your own professional journey, providing insight into your practices, strengths, and needs. At the classroom or program level, aggregate (or combined) data can show progress toward program outcomes for children and help staff identify professional development goals.

While teachers of infants and toddlers have a wealth of choices when it comes to collecting assessment information (see "Screenings and Other Formal Assessment Tools"), they most often rely on conducting and recording observations. These observations can happen quite naturally across the day—during everyday routines (drop-off and pickup, mealtimes, and nap times) and during play. This chapter focuses on the steps educators can take to understand and use the information they gather.

Screenings and Other Formal Assessment Tools

Teacher observations and documentation are usually informal ways of assessing infant and toddler learning and development. If concerns about a child's development arise—either from educators or the family—then a developmental screening may be in order. For example, if a toddler is consistently demonstrating repetitive behaviors, such as spinning or hand-flapping, further evaluation may be warranted.

Developmental screenings allow teachers and other professionals to formally compare a child's current skills and behaviors to a set of established norms. Screenings include the Ages & Stages

Questionnaires, BRIGANCE, and DENVER II, among others (Macy & Bagnato 2022). These screenings, typically administered by professionals outside the program, may indicate the need for a more comprehensive evaluation.

Screenings are designed to provide detailed information about a child's abilities and needs in a particular domain of development. Certain formal assessments can also be used for diagnostic purposes. Because consistent and accurate information is integral to early intervention/early special education efforts, early childhood educators can offer critical insights and details during the evaluation process.

Bringing Information to Life in Our Work

As Patricia McDonald (2018) writes, "Teachers are researchers, observing children to decide how to extend their learning both in the moment and by planning new play environments" (32). The observations infant and toddler teachers make can provide rich insights into the very young child's experiences, including:

> Their interests—where do their passions lie? (Are you seeing preferred actions and skills, like climbing or dancing? Or are the children using fine motor skills to work on puzzles, stack objects, or produce art? Are you seeing specific emerging interests, like dinosaurs or rolling items across the room or down ramps? Do you observe a child's curiosity, perhaps about how things work, as they explore a new toy in the classroom? Perhaps you notice pretend play themes like making dinner or taking care of pets.)

> Their development—are they showing early milestones toward walking (pulling up, creeping along furniture) or toileting (signaling when they are going to have a bowel movement)?

> Their needs—perhaps a 6-month-old cannot hold their bottle independently but can do so with support.

> Their temperament, likes, and dislikes—for example, some children may tolerate a block tower falling over and over again while others may be distressed the first time the blocks collapse.

Teachers can collect and record these observations in several ways. They may make a quick note on a sticky pad, take a video or photo, make a note in the child's chart or daily record, and/or record frequency counts of how often a specific behavior (like biting) is observed. Whatever system a teacher uses, it is important to partner with other staff in the setting so that everyone uses a similar approach.

DAP Observing infants and toddlers during play and noticing what children are doing and thinking during spontaneous conversations provides information teachers can use to plan curriculum and to respond sensitively during moment-to-moment interactions with children.

Regardless of how it is gathered, assessment information—including informal observation and other, more formal practices—is meaningful only when it is understood and brought to life in the early learning program. Educators can follow a three-step process to guide how they interpret and act on the information they collect.

1. Reflection: What Does It Mean?

Early childhood educators gather information about children for a variety of reasons. They may want to track a child's development, needs, and strengths; assess a program's compliance activities; or examine their own teaching practices and classroom climate. They can observe individual children or an entire class (which is particularly helpful when tracking progress toward a specific learning objective, such as adding new vocabulary to their repertoire, matching picture cards, responding to requests ["Can you give me one block?"], mastering physical skills like kicking a ball, or engaging in some peer play). Once they have gathered the information, they can connect with a supervisor or other staff member and family members (Scott-Little, with Reschke 2022). Reflection questions could include the following:

> What does this assessment information tell me about children's learning and development?

> What does it tell me about my teaching practices?

> What can I learn about the classroom climate, including how I interact with children and how they interact with each other? What biases of mine might it be revealing, and how are they affecting children?

> Does this information capture how children are accessing, mastering, and applying new knowledge and skills?

2. Feedback: What Is the Context?

There is a lot going on in an early learning program at any point in time, and that context may contribute to the "story" that observation and documentation tells. For example, perhaps an observation took place after a lockdown or fire drill, so children were more distressed and unsettled than usual. Or perhaps it occurred after a new staff member joined the classroom. When analyzing observations, consider these contexts and the ways they influence what you observe. This could prompt you to plan for additional observation.

Knowledge of the children (and families) in your setting is another important source of feedback. Consider how culture, language, background knowledge, immigration experiences, family strengths, and more influence children's learning. This intentional awareness of each child's unique context, strengths, and needs is aligned to developmentally appropriate practice: "The methods of assessment are responsive to the current developmental accomplishments, language(s), and experiences of young children. They recognize individual variation in learners and allow children to demonstrate their competencies in different ways" (NAEYC 2020a, 20).

3. Action Planning: What Comes Next?

Once you collect information, review it regularly to identify areas of growth and areas for attention or changes you may want to make. Based on your observations, you can design playful learning activities that are intentional and responsive to children's interests and abilities (Office of Head Start, ECLKC 2023a). When planning these activities, ask yourself the following questions (Peterson & Elam 2020):

> How can I set up the environment to better meet children's needs? Do I need to change routines, materials, or schedules?

> What milestones or learning objectives can I support through planned experiences?

> What resources or materials do I need to meet these objectives?

> Do I need to consider modifications, adaptations, or other adjustments to support each and every child's meaningful participation in learning experiences?

> What do families think their children should be learning right now? How can I include families in goal setting for their children? How am I communicating with families about the learning experiences children are receiving in the classroom?

For example, imagine that observations over time showed that teachers were engaging in fewer conversations with emergent multilingual learners than with monolingual children (Hannon 2019). Seeing these data, teachers might assign a group of children to each staff member in the room, with the goal that adults engage each of their children in multiple conversations a day. Teaching teams, with the support of a coach or reflective supervisor, could take time to consider what issues are behind these differences in engaging with children; together, they could map out the intentional use of strategies to support an increase in conversations with multilingual learners and plan for a future data collection to monitor improvement. At the program level, directors might decide to invest in professional development that focuses on enriching classroom language environments for multilingual children.

Informal observations can also guide adult learning by providing an opportunity for teachers to reflect and consider their own professional strengths and needs. After implementing any changes, educators can plan to collect follow-up data: Did the adjustments lead to anticipated outcomes? If not, why? Is more time needed to implement the changes, or should teachers try other approaches instead?

Observation and Documentation in Action

The following vignette shows how Gabriella used the three-step process in her infant and toddler classroom:

Many children in Gabriella's class struggle with transitions, particularly when the toddlers prepare to go outside. She asks her colleague, Isis, to come in and observe during this time of day. Isis sees that some children are zipped up and standing by the door while other children are waiting to be helped into their jackets. By the time children get outside, some are crying, others have unzipped their jackets, and one pushes a peer to get out the door.

At a follow-up meeting with Isis, Gabriella uses the three-step approach of reflection, feedback, and action planning. She *reflects* on her frustration that a seemingly "simple" transition poses such a challenge, then considers the observational data that some children are waiting up to four to five minutes in their jackets and boots by the door. Gabriella explains that her goal is making the transition to the playground smoother for everyone. With Isis's help, Gabriella considers important *feedback* about the children she works with—young toddlers have difficulty waiting, yet they need adult assistance with dressing. Gabriella then focuses on *action planning*: What can be done to ease this transition?

Gabriella and her two coteachers decide to put the children's coats on the backs of their chairs during snack time and to line up boots by the playground door. As the first children finish their snack, Gabriella will help them get dressed, and her two coteachers will take them to the playground. One coteacher will stay to supervise outdoor play while the other heads back to the classroom. Gabriella will remain in the room, helping each child put on jacket and boots, while her coteacher leads children to the playground individually or in small groups as they're ready. This approach cuts down children's waiting time, allows for more one-on-one attention, creates opportunities for children to practice early dressing skills, and ultimately meets Gabriella's goal of providing a calmer transition to outdoor play.

NEXT STEPS

> As you review assessment information for your setting or practice, take a moment to check in with yourself. Do you have any immediate reactions (pride, satisfaction, insecurity, frustration)? It is normal to have strong feelings about assessment data. Acknowledging our feelings helps us manage them so these reactions don't get in the way of our ability to use and learn from the information.

> Look at data as a snapshot in time and one piece of a larger picture. Consider what other sources of information you may have that can add to this picture. Informal observations, children's work samples, videos, and feedback from families are all examples of other important data sources.

> Use assessment information as a jumping-off point for curriculum planning. Experiment with new approaches, routines, or activities with children, allowing enough time for these new ways to have an effect. Invite a colleague to observe you implementing these changes and to offer thoughts on how they're working.

> Share assessment information with families to help them understand planned changes to the environment or your teaching (see "Sharing Assessment Information with Families" on page 50). For example, you might use a weekly newsletter to explain that you've been observing young toddlers stacking objects and knocking them down. Let families know that, in the coming weeks, you'll

introduce different types of blocks and boxes to give children an opportunity to explore this cause-and-effect relationship with a range of materials. Ask them if they've noticed their child engaging in similar cause-and-effect behaviors.

Sharing Assessment Information with Families

Observations are rich "moments in time" and can offer families a deeper understanding of what their children do and discover during the day. By sharing these observations during pickup time, in classroom newsletters, or during family-educator conferences, teachers can build trust and connections with the families in their settings.

Families have a right to understand what information is being collected about their children, how the information is being used, and in what ways it is being shared with other staff and agencies. Because assessment can be formal or informal, specific to one child or program-wide, educators may struggle with how to meaningfully share the information they gather. Here are some guidelines for discussing data collection (Lin et al. 2016):

> Inform families about the program's assessment practices at enrollment. Explain what information the program collects, why they collect it, and how it may be used.

> Allow families to choose if they want to share personal information. This helps build trust. Programs should also outline the ways they ensure families' privacy and the data protections they have in place (such as confidentiality agreements, data sharing agreements, and secure data storage).

> Highlight the benefits of collecting assessment information. These include determining a child's eligibility for community services, documenting that children are receiving necessary services, illustrating a child's progress and learning across the curriculum, ensuring compliance with funding agencies, and guiding improvements to the program.

Conclusion

While most often informal, teacher and staff observations are an important contribution to effective teaching. Taking the time to understand and apply these findings creates an environment of ongoing reflection and learning—for teachers and children.

REBECCA PARLAKIAN, MA, is the senior director of programs at Zero to Three. She has coauthored five parenting and professional curricula and published articles on topics ranging from dual language development to the impact of screens on very young children.

CHAPTER 10

Observation and Documentation
Both Art and Science

Malori-Naomi Wallace-Wyche

Observation and documentation are both artistic and scientific works that teachers engage in each day. Through these processes, educators discover and share knowledge about children with families, colleagues, other community members, and the children themselves (Edwards, Gandini, & Forman 2012). As educators observe and document children's language and actions and reflect on what these indicate about children's learning, they think intentionally about the design of their settings, the materials they select, and their day-to-day practice. In a way, teachers are curators of educational experiences for young children. They are aided in this work through the artifacts and evidence they collect, which come together to support deeper understandings of children and child development (Parlakian 2023).

Over time, these processes of observation and documentation build on each other, leading to more discoveries and deepening improving teaching practices. In this chapter, I explore how considering observation and documentation as both artistic and scientific processes can support teachers in thinking about their purposes for assessment and integrating intentional teaching practices into conversations and interactions with children, colleagues, and others outside the classroom walls.

Defining the Processes of Observation and Documentation

Observing children well requires intention, attention, and openness to the ways that children's development and learning can and will surprise you. After and as you observe, you document. Documentation, or the process of pulling observations together and presenting them in a way that shows and reflects the children's learning and growth, both results from and informs observation. With time, observation and documentation can support teachers in adapting an existing curriculum or developing an emergent curriculum that intentionally focuses on the children's interests and curiosities, fosters their inquiry and active engagement, and uses documentation as a way to communicate about learning (Sampson & McLean 2021). As children continue to build on previous experiences, observation and documentation become increasingly active and dynamic, encouraging teachers to create additional hands-on experiences based on observing how much children are engaging with certain activities or materials. Teachers document what they observe during the new experiences, and the process continues on and on. In the following sections, I invite you delve deeper into the concepts of observations and documentation. My aim is to inspire you to see these processes as both artistic expression and evidence-based professional practice.

Planning and facilitating effective emergent curriculum require a great deal of skill. While all teachers can be responsive to children's interests and provide additional information and resources for exploration, more complex emergent curriculum projects require advanced planning, a specific sequence of steps and processes, consideration of goals, and the knowledgeable oversight of an experienced teacher. Educators can build on their current practices and, over time, begin to incorporate more complex projects.

Observation: A Scientific Meeting of Curious Minds

Observation is intentional and focused on children's development. Observing differs from supervising due to the nature of what educators are looking for. Supervision is concerned with children's health and safety. As teachers supervise, they ensure that children engage in play in ways that are appropriate and not dangerous to themselves or others. This is valuable and necessary, but it is not enough. Observing children as they interact with materials, ideas, peers, and adults requires an intentional shift from considering merely if actions are safe or appropriate to *how* the actions, interactions, and language of the children *contribute to their growth and development*. You practice the skill of observation every time you are intentional about studying how a child is learning. It requires an awareness of and confidence in the competency of all children. Educators have to hold the perspective that children are co-constructors of their knowledge and are, always, involved in the wondrous process of learning.

Like other scientific endeavors, observation is geared toward investigation. Educators ask questions about children's learning and development. These questions help them focus their observations and identify their own curiosities about children and teaching strategies. For example, teachers might wonder, "What will happen if I give these toddlers scissors and paper?" In response to this curiosity, they might provide scissors and paper at an art table, give toddlers time to use the materials, and watch closely as the children rip, cut, arrange, and rearrange the paper. This instance is just one example of how teachers' wonderings and children's curiosity and eagerness to engage can transform into a meeting of their minds through materials and experiences. That is, teachers engage children's minds and senses through providing materials and facilitating the use of these materials and, in doing so, teachers satisfy and extend their own curiosity about and awareness of what children know and can do. Having done this, teachers can also use what they discover to think about how to facilitate further exploration of those materials. It takes time for children to build skills, and teachers' close observation and thoughtful questions help them know how best to support children on their ways to mastery.

Building Knowledge and Building Upon Knowledge: Research-Informed Observation

During observations, educators draw on their knowledge of research and science—the backbone of this process—to inform their interpretations of the learning that is happening and to inform their actions and the ways they support children (Scott-Little, with Reschke 2020). When teachers understand, for example, how children's social skills develop and the importance of schemas, they become attuned to the myriad ways children are developing and begin to see this development in their observations of the everyday. Here are just two examples:

> When educators see children attempting to negotiate turn taking and support them in sharing their voices with one another, they are witnessing social learning and attachment theories unfold in real time (Ho & Funk 2018). In addition, children can see that they will have adults there to provide support when they need it—the basis for secure, trusting relationships (Li & Ramirez 2023).

> When children are at work building castles and zoos with blocks, educators are watching as children use and develop schemas that reflect and inform their understanding of the world. Schema theory explains that children recognize related concepts and features of sensory experiences and internalize their understandings and actions based on these patterns (Brierley 2018).

Observation highlights for educators the ways children are constantly promoting their own growth and development. It also reveals children's developing understandings of concepts, sheds light on their engagement with materials, and informs teachers' curricular planning.

For example, returning to the scissors and paper above, you might ask: When provided with scissors and paper, do the children enjoy the cutting motion or do they become curious about the scraps of paper falling on the floor? Do they attempt to cut or rip paper? When they do so, do they use one hand or both? How successful are they? Another possibility is that children are spending more time examining the scissors and how they are designed than the paper.

Any one of these observations could lead you down the path of an entirely different investigation if you are willing to be led by your observations.

Curating Learning Materials: A Scientific *and* Artistic Response to Observation

After close observation rooted in curiosity, curating learning materials is a crucial step in the meeting of minds between teachers and children. This careful curation is, first, a response to initial curiosity; second, a chance for educators to assess and observe particular phenomena; and third, an artistic and creative process for educators. If an observation is rooted in an initial curiosity that yields a research question, then the inclusion of carefully considered materials in the learning environment is the educator's research experiment. Teachers create the invitation and select the materials to foster intentional moments where, returning to observation, they again assess children's growth and learning. For example, as teachers provide children with materials, space, and time, they create opportunities to observe the following skills:

> **Problem solving:** Can the children find a productive way to engage with the materials?

> **Physical development:** Do the children have the motor skills to be able to use the materials?

> **Negotiation:** Can the children independently use verbal and/or nonverbal communication to share, take turns, and help each other? Do the children, with assistance, use verbal and/or nonverbal communication to share, take turns, and help each other?

> **Cognitive development:** Through what means do children seek to solve problems and engage in challenges, to seek knowledge for themselves? What steps have they taken to further their understanding of materials and/or information shared with them?

> **Creativity:** How did the children use the materials in new and inventive ways?

Creating invitations is also an artistic process that involves considering everything from the quality of the materials to the aesthetics of their physical layout. It is an opportunity for educators to get creative and to try new things that they feel will be responsive to the unique children in their classroom.

The goal of this intentional curation is to provide children with opportunities to explore so that teachers can focus on observation while maintaining supervision. Children need time and space to touch, hear, see, smell, and even taste depending on the particulars of the learning experience. Teachers also need space to begin the process of recording their observations. This recording, documentation, is the focus of the next section.

Illustrating Process: The Intention and Beauty of Documentation

Documentation refers to the process of distilling and creating a legible display that illustrates children's learning and development. Documentation also refers to the product or artifact that is the result of this distilling. As they observe children and curate

materials in response to those observations, teachers enter into the process of capturing and reflecting on photos, videos, transcribed conversations, and discussions and interactions that occurred during the learning experience. In documentation, teachers gather traces of information about children that are informed by children's interests and teachers' curiosities (Edwards, Gandini, & Forman 2012). Like a scientist does with data or a curator does with art, so a teacher gathers these pieces into a collection that has meaning and presents them in a way that is both beautiful and informative. The collection that results is documentation as a product.

Documentation is most clearly an artistic process and product when it seeks to and is created with a mind toward inviting audiences—families, colleagues, children, and the broader community—to look at it.

While documentation can take many different forms (Stacey 2018), beautiful or aesthetically pleasing documentation has great potential to stimulate the learning of both children and adults.

An aesthetically pleasing and informative presentation provides images that allow children, colleagues, and families to see the children playing, creating, exploring materials, and engaging in the various routines of the day. Rich documentation pairs these images with evidence—typically written captions informed by and based in research and theory—that details how this material, interaction, or experience contributes to children's development.

Documentation as a product is a visually engaging attempt at sharing some possible answers to the questions raised by teacher researchers. The goal of documenting these processes is to provide insight into how learning experiences met the goals the teachers had for the children and to provide information educators and families can use to better support children's development and learning. Documentation displays records and makes visible the results of children's inquiries—and they can also raise new questions and lead educators and children further into inquiry.

To return yet again to the previous example of providing scissors and paper for the toddlers, imagine that the documentation panel of the children's explorations reveals that the children, even though they enjoyed the scissors, ended up casting them aside and instead ripping the paper. Moving forward, the teacher might explore the children's responses to different textures of paper or support them in exploring either adhesive materials such as white glue, glue sticks, or masking tape or other materials such as tongs or droppers that give children similar opportunities to develop fine motor skills and yet involve a different way of engaging with paper.

Presented in a way that shows the process of children's exploration and teacher reflection and also invites others to reflect on the process, a documentation panel has the potential to engage, inspire, and inform.

What Teachers and Others Gain from Documentation

One of the foremost purposes of documentation is to promote an awareness of the importance of early childhood education within the community. Families, educators, and other adults need to see children's learning made concrete and have opportunities to connect the principles of development to their daily interactions and work with children. Educators use documentation to make visible the science behind child development in ways that encourage and inspire. For example, a growing understanding of how play promotes learning and development may help adults embrace play as a developmentally appropriate and beneficial practice and to imagine some ways to invite more play into their work with children. Families and other adults in the community then become partners with educators and can advocate for developmentally appropriate practices in their communities.

Documentation is also valuable for children! When teachers share documentation with children, even with infants and toddlers, children have rich opportunities to see themselves creating, playing, developing, and growing. This can inspire children to build on previous knowledge, persevere in developing new and emergent competencies, and more than anything help them feel seen for who they are and what they can do. In this way, documentation—a process that blends and integrates artistic dispositions with scientific systematicity—supports children in developing a positive view of themselves. As you move forward in your work, I encourage you to continue to seek new discoveries and to amplify your artistry.

MALORI-NAOMI WALLACE-WYCHE (she/they) is an early childhood educator and alumni member of John Hopkins School of Education and the City Teaching Alliance. Her pedagogy involves the use of emergent curriculum with influences from Reggio Emilia and Montessori.

CHAPTER 11

Using a Child-Centered Approach to Shift from a Deficit Mindset

Julia Luckenbill, Aarti Subramaniam, and Janet Thompson

Zenobia joined the toddler room when she was 24 months old. She had a major birth trauma and exhibits developmental delays in language and gross motor skills. Including Zenobia in the classroom means working closely with her family and her occupational therapist to provide appropriate play experiences. With support, Zenobia is able to join her peers in activities such as art. She loves playdough and water play, and participating in these activities gives her a space where she can join in parallel play with the other children.

Teachers Hannah and Shelby adapt gross motor experiences such as climbing by staying close to Zenobia and coaching her. They also provide alternative ways she can be successful, like using the simpler stairs to get up the climber, while peers use the more complex rock wall. All of the toddlers in the room use gestures and speech to communicate, so Zenobia's language delay is easily accommodated, and she can use gestures or words to join peers in play. Hannah and Shelby observe that Zenobia is a valued member of the toddler community (rather than excluded for her differences) and that she is often invited into play with the other children. One memorable day, she races down from the loft while several other toddlers stand at the bottom, waving flags and cheering for her.

Zenobia's teachers use observation, reflection, and individualized teaching to create inclusive and joyful learning experiences. Using a child-centered approach, they view Zenobia as a child first, and as a child who has a delay, disability, or other need second. In the same way, instead of including "a Down syndrome child" in your program, you include Melissa, who has Down syndrome. With this mindset, you can examine the many ways that Melissa can play across the developmental domains. This helps you focus on what a child can do and leads to discoveries: that the child is very capable, even surpassing other children their age in some activities, such as showing empathy during peer interactions or connecting with you in games like peekaboo. In other play activities, they may need more support, such as dressing up, climbing, and/or verbal communication so their peers can understand how the child wants to play. As you join the child in play and work hand in hand with their family and therapists on ways to support them, you'll observe the child's growing skills and confidence and celebrate their competencies.

Adapting Experiences to Meet Children's Unique Needs

While a child's interests and abilities may differ from those of their peers, you can adapt experiences to be age appropriate while supporting the child's interests (perhaps in shaking, mouthing, and banging things). This allows the child to join in with age-mates in the same activities. For example, if all the children enjoy shaking instruments to music, add shaker eggs to make this an inclusive experience for a child who is in the toddler room and whose interests or skills are developmentally more suited to the infant room.

You may have infants or toddlers in your room who do not have a disability but who need your focused support for other reasons. A child with a background of abuse or neglect or who has undergone extensive hospitalization, for example, may not initially seek you out for play or feel comfortable playing in the classroom. For this child, you may need to design a special time together or focus on one-on-one play and coaching to help them learn that the classroom is a place where they can trust and feel safe.

For dual language learners, communicating in their home languages is key to their comfort and success in the classroom. In Xiao Ming's case (below), there were student teachers in the program who spoke his language:

> Xiao Ming joined the toddler room when he was 25 months old. He speaks only Mandarin and until recently has lived in China with his grandparents. At first, he seems too afraid to play, but his patient Mandarin-speaking student teachers discover his passion for airplanes, art, and nature. Using this knowledge, they design play experiences for him. They put plastic airplanes on the shelf, include water play in the garden, and join him in harvesting celery and tasting it. These moments of shared focus on his play and interests lead to longer periods of relaxed play in the block area and yard, and over time he is able to engage his peers in activities such as bubble blowing and digging a group hole, even using a few words of English with them. Key to his success are the teachers who are willing to use words in his home language.

Your program may not have a staff member or student who speaks a child's home language. Work with families and community partners to find someone who can, and learn some words in the language yourself, even if just a few.

EQUITY Scaffolding children's learning to achieve meaningful goals means setting challenging but achievable goals for each child and building on their strengths and interests. Teachers provide supports as needed and communicate authentic confidence in each child's ability to achieve these goals.

Facilitating Play with Other Children

Children with delays or disabilities sometimes struggle to enter play with their peers. This can be due to a physical barrier such as being unable to hear play cues, a physical challenge like struggling to keep up with other toddlers pushing carts quickly on the bike path, or social challenges like finding it uncomfortable to make eye contact or be in close physical interactions with others. You must be a play coach for children, becoming the bridge for connection and offering tips

for interaction. For example, you might stay close by to point out social cues to a child and his peers: "Look, Rashid, Oliver is smiling at you. I think he likes it when you play chase. I bet he'd like to do it again."

Look for ways to include *all* children in your classroom culture. Encourage everyone to learn a few signs to use with a child with hearing loss. Provide dress-up items with many ways to fasten them. In addition to providing paint and other sensory experiences at a table surface, use easels children can stand at, which lets them make larger arm movements that are easier to control than the smaller hand muscles. Design the classroom to invite exploration in different ways and at multiple levels.

Customizing Your Toolkit to Each Child

You'll try out many new tools to help all children as they develop play skills, supporting each one as they become increasingly capable. Each child who joins your community is unique, deserving of an individualized, responsive approach. You have an important role to play as you adapt to their needs and create an individualized yet communal space to grow, play, and learn.

How do you do this?

> **Observe and document children's interactions** (Parlakian 2023). Pay attention to skills that come easily and those that present a challenge. Take note of adaptations that have been successful and those that were ineffective. Keep a daily log to record accomplishments with dates and details that can be shared with families. Use the notes to identify additional skills that need support and add related activities to planning.

> **Use quality assessments to help design experiences** (Zollitsch & Dean 2010). Begin by paying close attention, observing and documenting a child's activities, emotions, interactions, abilities, and achievements. You can use a high-quality child assessment tool designed for use with infants and toddlers, such as California's Desired Results Developmental Profile (DRDP), or tools designed to work with widely used curriculum frameworks for infants and toddlers, such as the Teaching Strategies GOLD assessment system or HighScope's COR Advantage. This helps to keep your

documentation broad based, objective, and built on a child's own play activities in the early learning setting. Once you have gathered the information you need and considered which skills might be emerging next, you can design experiences and strategies to support those skills.

> **Apply your personal experience and knowledge of developmentally appropriate practice along with insights gained from families** (Kinsner 2022). Recognize that your expertise lies in the knowledge of child development and your ability to observe, reflect, and adapt as you actively engage with children in their daily activities and support new skills through your curriculum and interactions. While evaluation, diagnosis, appropriate labeling of developmental differences, and specific therapeutic strategies are the job of medical and early intervention specialists—and it's vital to work closely with them where possible—reflect on your own interactions with children and build on your conversations with families to refine and support the learning and development of all infants and toddlers. Consider the approach these teachers took to include a child with complex medical needs in the classroom:

LeShawn and his family joined the infant room when he was 11 months old. LeShawn's gastrointestinal condition was diagnosed at birth, and he spent his early life in the hospital undergoing multiple painful procedures and nearly died.

Including LeShawn in the program has meant learning about his G-tube and specialized feeding needs and how to handle his deep (and realistic) distrust of nonfamily. (Most strangers in the hospital smile while causing pain, a confusing message for infants who are learning to trust others.)

The teachers have found that including an 11-month-old in the program with the motor and feeding skills of a 3-month-old but the cognitive skills typical of his age was not a challenge. They already serve nonmobile infants who need staff to assist in feeding, and they can bring age-appropriate curriculum items to LeShawn's side and join him as he explores them. Designing curriculum for LeShawn includes adding medical play props to the classroom so he can act out his very real fears and, through play, master his feelings about real medical tools. The teachers are also aware that he is very sensitive to touch, as he often gets distraught when peers brush or bump into

him during play. With coaching, the other toddlers have begun to notice his tears and will help calm him, bringing his family's photograph or singing to him. The empathy he has helped everyone develop, families and children alike, is a gift.

Including children with diverse abilities in your classroom community is indeed a gift for everyone. You will find yourself stretching and growing, trying different ways of doing things, and adding new skills to your teaching toolkit as you help children join in the play in meaningful ways. Working with those who are specialists in a child's disability may teach you new ways to engage the child's peers and support children who do not qualify for special services but who need more support. Although inclusion does often involve extra work, both in documenting learning and in designing curriculum, the reward of seeing every child thrive and grow, taking on new play challenges every day, makes the process incredibly worthwhile.

JULIA LUCKENBILL, MA, is the director at the Danbury location of Davis Parent Nursery School in Davis, California, and coaches parents through the Davis Joint Unified School District Adult Education program.

AARTI SUBRAMANIAM, PhD, is a research analyst for the University of California Agriculture and Natural Resources 4-H youth development program.

JANET THOMPSON, MA, is the former director of the Early Childhood Laboratory at the University of California, Davis, Center for Child and Family Studies.

Resources for Teachers and Families

> "Creating Inclusive Environments and Learning Experiences for Infants and Toddlers," Child Care Technical Assistance Network. https://childcareta .acf.hhs.gov/resource/creating-inclusive -environments-and-learning-experiences-infants -and-toddlers

> "Culturally Responsive Care," Infant/Toddler Resource Guide, Child Care Technical Assistance Network. https://childcareta.acf.hhs.gov/infant -toddler-resource-guide/pd-ta-professionals/ relationship-based-care/culturally-responsive

> "Promoting Inclusion in Infant and Toddler Settings," by Rebecca Parlakian (*Young Children*, Vol. 76, No. 4, pp. 90–94, Winter 2021). NAEYC .org/resources/pubs/yc/winter2021/inclusion -infant-toddler

> "Supporting Emergent Bilingual Children in Early Learning," Education Development Center. www.edc.org/sites/default/files/uploads/ Supporting-Emergent-Bilingual-Children _English.pdf

> "Supporting Medically Fragile Children and Their Families," Julia Luckenbill & Amy Zide (*Young Children*, Vol. 72, No. 4, pp. 79–84, September 2017). NAEYC.org/resources/pubs/yc/sep2017/ supporting-medically-fragile-children

Empowering Infants' and Toddlers' Learning Through Scaffolding

Linda Groves Gillespie and Jan D. Greenberg

Ms. Tonya plays peekaboo with Anthony, 4 months old. She holds a blanket in front of her face, peeks out over the top of it, and says, "Peekaboo!" Anthony laughs. After she does this a few times, she notices that Anthony's attention has waned. The next time she puts the blanket up, she moves it to the side of her face and peeks out from a different place. Anthony looks surprised and laughs, reengaged.

• • • • • • • • • • • • •

Shayla, 11 months old, lets go of the cart she is pushing and stands alone. Her teacher, Mr. Peter, is sitting nearby and says, "Hi, Shayla!" He reaches his hand toward her, and she takes one step, then another, then falls down. Shayla's eyes open wide, and Mr. Peter says, "Boom, you fell down, but you're okay. Do you want to try again?" Shayla reaches up her arms, and Mr. Peter helps her stand up. He holds her hands while she steadies herself, then gives her two small toys to hold so that she balances on her own. He says, "Okay, Shayla, can you walk to me?" Holding tightly to the two toys, she takes three steps and reaches Mr. Peter right before she falls down. "You did it!" Mr. Peter exclaims.

• • • • • • • • • • • • •

Twenty-two-month-old Aydin has just arrived at Ms. Evelyn's family child care home. Ms. Evelyn has three other toddlers close to Aydin's age. Recently, she has noticed that Aydin knows the color yellow. She places several yellow objects on a small table, along with a few red objects. Aydin immediately goes to the table and picks up a yellow block, saying, "Lellow!" Ms. Evelyn says, "Yes, that's a yellow block. Can you find something else yellow?" Aydin looks back at the table and picks up a yellow toy car. He brings it to Ms. Evelyn, saying, "Lellow!"

Each of these scenarios shows skilled teachers setting up environments and facilitating infants' and toddlers' development and learning. Their process is called *scaffolding*. Scaffolding is how adults support children's development and learning by offering just the right help at just the right time in just the right way. As children begin to master the skill, scaffolding is gradually reduced and changed to support the next learning opportunity (NAEYC, n.d.). While the use of scaffolding is typically associated with older children, adults' natural interactions with infants and toddlers are scaffolding learning all the time. Understanding the process can help educators be more intentional in their interactions as they become more sensitive to the many opportunities to scaffold presented in everyday interactions.

Exploring the Benefits of Scaffolding

Scaffolding allows children to solve a problem or carry out a task that is beyond their current abilities. It is a bridge teachers create to connect existing knowledge to new knowledge and understanding. Successful scaffolding happens in what Lev Vygotsky (1978), a pioneering psychologist, called the *zone of proximal development* (ZPD). The ZPD is the difference between what a person can do and learn on their own and what they can do and learn with the help of someone who is more experienced. As a result, scaffolding is collaborative in nature. To provide scaffolding, teachers need to join infants and toddlers in play and build from there. Scaffolding requires several considerations: understanding children's overall development; understanding the ways individual children approach learning; establishing realistic learning objectives; and matching strategies to each child's current interests, knowledge, and skills.

For example, in the peekaboo scenario, Ms. Tonya sensitively models how to play, but she also adjusts her play to match Anthony's interest and attention. By slightly changing the game, she reengages Anthony and holds his attention a little longer. This type of play not only encourages active participation in a game but also increases learning.

One in-depth three-teacher study demonstrated the many potential benefits of teachers scaffolding development by joining infants' play in sensitive and responsive ways (Jung & Recchia 2013). These teachers were able to empower and enhance the self-motivation of the infants in their care. In the earlier scenarios in this chapter, each teacher joined a child's play and extended learning through careful observation, supportive environments, and active engagement. These strategies facilitated the children's abilities to learn a little more than what they might have learned on their own.

Some research studies (see, e.g., Dahl et al. 2017 and Dahl, Goeltz, & Brownell 2022) show how scaffolding plays an important role in infants' emerging prosocial skills such as helping. Prosocial skills such as caring, comforting, compassion, and cooperating (Chutabhakdikul 2020) are critical competencies that enable children to build and maintain relationships with others. Such skills are connected to children's engagement in play with adults and other children; "helping" tasks such handing an object that is out of reach to another person or cleaning up are often done within a play context. The earlier scenario with Mr. Peter demonstrates how sensitive scaffolding can also be a model for caring, comforting, and "helping" behaviors within a play situation.

DAP Providing the right amount and type of scaffolding requires knowledge of child development and learning in general and deep personal knowledge of each child. Teachers expand their understanding through close observation of children and by learning from the families.

How teachers view infants may influence how they approach scaffolding. The teachers who participated in the in-depth three-teacher study saw infants as innately motivated and competent. They carefully observed the babies' individual temperaments—how they liked to play; when they gave up; in what ways they liked to receive teacher support; how responsive and sensitive they were to teacher actions; how enthusiastic they were in their play; and to what

degree they maintained their focus in play. This careful and intentional observing enabled the teachers to sensitively individualize their scaffolding to meet each infant's needs.

Similar observations and responsiveness are apparent in the opening scenarios. Anthony maintained his attention and joint play because Ms. Tonya slightly changed where she peeked out from behind the blanket. Shayla took a few more steps because Mr. Peter responded sensitively to her attempts to walk by providing props (toys) that helped her balance. And Ms. Evelyn prepared her environment based on her previous experiences with Aydin's interest in the color yellow. Each teacher also allowed the children enough space to pursue their interests through play and supported learning by being present and actively engaged.

 EQUITY Offer meaningful, relevant, and appropriately challenging activities to *all* children, across all interests and abilities. As you provide the supports a child needs, communicate—both verbally and nonverbally—your authentic confidence in the child's ability to achieve the challenging yet achievable goals you set.

Observing, Reflecting, and Responding to Children

Reaffirming the large research base on scaffolding (see, e.g., Office of Head Start, ECKLC 2022 and 2023c), the in-depth three-teacher study highlights how observing and reflecting help teachers to better understand each infant's preferences, culture, and what support they may need to move forward. Providing that support in just the right context—or, to use Vygotsky's term, within each infant's zone of proximal development—leads to more effective scaffolding. Some of the effective strategies the researchers identified include

› Modeling for children

› Encouraging children in verbal and nonverbal ways

› Following the child's lead

> Physical intervention, such as providing assistance with new skills

> Offering and accepting choices

> Joining in a child's play as a partner while still allowing the child to lead

An important part of observing and reflecting to better understand and respond to infants and toddlers is two-way communication with children's families. Families know their children best—"their temperaments, personalities, strengths, vulnerabilities, talents, and special needs" (Office of Head Start, ECKLC 2023b). Learning about each child from their family helps you know what the child is doing at home and the kinds of support they offer when their child is learning a new skill. You also have valuable information to share with families about what you see the child do and the kinds of support you provide. The strategies mentioned earlier are ones families may already be doing with their child—and ones you might offer families to try! This two-way communication strengthens your partnerships with families and the home-school connection, which is vital for infants and toddlers.

Try It

To get started with scaffolding, try these suggestions:

> Pick a child to watch during free play and consider these guiding questions.

- What do you think the child is trying to learn through play?

- What temperament characteristics do you see the child displaying?

- What do you see as your role in supporting the child's learning?

- What strategies do you want to use to support that learning?

> Choose a strategy to try with the child you observed. How did the child respond? What else did you notice? Would this child benefit from more occasions when you try this strategy, or might you try something different another time?

> Take turns observing fellow teachers supporting children's learning. Document which scaffolding strategies they use.

Teachers of infants and toddlers shape the curriculum by carefully setting up the environment and by watching and wondering about children's current interests and abilities. They act on those observations by extending each child's learning through playful interactions and scaffolding. In this way, teachers set the stage for children's future learning and success!

LINDA GROVES GILLESPIE, MS, retired from Zero to Three, has worked in the field of early education for the past 40 years, providing professional development about the importance of the first three years of life.

JAN D. GREENBERG, MA, is a senior manager of content quality with the National Center on Early Childhood Development, Teaching, and Learning in Washington, DC. She develops, reviews, and provides feedback on training materials and resources to support education services in Head Start programs serving infants, toddlers, and preschoolers.

CHAPTER 13

What Babies Ask of Us
Contexts to Support Learning About Self and Other

Mary Jane Maguire-Fong

According to noted educator Vivian Gussin Paley (2011), "Two questions predominate in the minds of young children: 'Where's my family?' and 'Who's my friend?'" In few words, Paley, author of 13 insightful books that illuminate children's social and emotional competence, captured the essence of what young children ask of us with respect to social and emotional support.

Paley listened with great care to children as they played. In return, they revealed to her their quest to make sense of strong feelings and to make friends. Carlina Rinaldi, former president of Reggio Children and pedagogical director of the Reggio Emilia Infant-Toddler Centers and Preschools, echoes this idea when she advises, "The most important verbs in educational practice are no longer 'to talk,' 'to explain' or 'to transmit'—but 'to listen'" (2006b, 126). Magda Gerber, the inspirational founder of Resources for Infant Educarers, elaborates further in saying, "Let go of all other issues that wander through your mind and really pay attention. . . . Infants do not yet speak our language but they give us many, many signs" (2002, 6).

Teaching and learning, when working with infants and toddlers, begins with observing and listening with care. Throughout the day, infants strive to make sense of all they encounter, including a wide array of strong feelings:

> The tender moments of sadness when family members depart, leaving them behind

> The unsettling conflicts spawned as one toddler lashes out in anger when another grabs away a toy

> The silent, curious dialogue that transpires as two 12-month-olds sit near each other, one watching the other explore a toy

> The look of excitement and anticipation on a baby's face in a game of peekaboo

Infants Are Highly Aware of Others

Researchers who study infants and toddlers carefully observe them, with fascinating results that give insight into how infants "know" others (Reddy 2008; Reddy et al. 2019). An infant just a few hours old, when held face-to-face, will imitate a researcher's facial gesture, such as a protruding tongue (Nagy et al. 2013). When researchers show infants scenes with puppets—in which some puppets act in ways that help others and some act in ways that hinder others—infants appear to distinguish between behavior that helps and behavior that hurts (Hamlin 2013). For example, 5- to 12- month-old infants were shown a scene in which a puppet tries but fails to open a box. In the next scene, a different puppet pops up and helps the first puppet open the box. The babies were shown the original scene again, but this time a third puppet pops up and flops down hard on top of the box, preventing the box from being opened. When researchers showed the infants a tray holding a choice of two puppets (the puppet that helped and the puppet that hindered), overwhelmingly, infants chose the puppet that helped (Hamlin & Wynn 2011).

In another series of experiments, researchers observed that when toddlers watched someone who appeared to need help, they often tried to assist them (Hepach et al. 2023; Warneken & Tomasello 2007). For example, when toddlers watched as a researcher silently struggled with the simple task of opening a cabinet door while balancing a stack of books, most toddlers moved to assist within 10 seconds, walking to the cabinet and opening the door. In another study, toddlers watched as a researcher pinned clothes on a clothesline. The researcher accidentally dropped a clothespin, and although the researcher made no request for help, most of the 18-month-olds retrieved and returned the clothespin to the researcher. However, when the researcher intentionally threw the clothespin to the floor as the toddler watched, the toddler did not retrieve the thrown object.

These investigations are part of a growing body of research detailing babies' emerging understanding of others' feelings and intentions. Key findings demonstrate that infants

> Are biologically prepared to seek out and interact joyfully with companions (Endevelt-Shapira & Feldman 2023; Trevarthen & Bjørkvold 2016)

> Expect social partners to respond in kind to their gaze, smile, or vocalization (Reddy et al. 2019)

> Appear to assess people's actions and vocalizations as to safety or threat, helpful or hurtful (Margoni & Surian 2018; Ruba, Meltzoff, & Repacholi 2021)

This image of infants as highly aware of others' intentions and feelings challenges a long-held assumption that children under age 3 are *egocentric,* meaning that they have difficulty seeing others' perspectives or needs. In fact, more recent evidence suggests the opposite—infants are more inclined to be *allocentric,* meaning that they are biologically prepared to be aware of and concerned with others' movements, orientation, and feelings, and they are eager to engage with and imitate others (Trevarthen & Delafield-Butt 2017). In short, infants come into the world actively making meaning of people.

The Three Contexts for Learning

In social play and interaction with others, infants learn the conventions, skills, and concepts valued in the culture that surrounds them (Rogoff 2003). As active makers of meaning, infants ask those who care for them to respect their competence and to support their efforts to engage with others and to cope with strong feelings that often emerge as they do so. As Rinaldi (2006a, 21) explains, "Children ask us to see them as scientists or philosophers searching to understand something, to draw out a meaning. . . . We are asked to be the child's traveling companion in this search for meaning."

J. Ronald Lally (2009, 52), who served as the codirector of the WestEd Center for Child and Family Studies, built on Rinaldi's sage advice when he wrote, "The most critical curriculum components are no longer seen as lessons and lesson plans but rather the planning of settings and experiences that allow learning to take place." When caring for a group of infants or toddlers, there are three such settings, or *contexts for learning* (Maguire-Fong 2020). One context is the *play space,* thoughtfully prepared and provisioned to support the inquisitive infant or toddler. A second context involves the *daily routines* of care, like diapering, meals, dressing, and preparing for nap. Each routine is an excellent opportunity to invite infants and toddlers to use emerging skills and concepts. The third context occurs within everyday *conversations and interactions*, like the stories and songs teachers share with young children or the guidance they offer with respect to children's behavior.

Play Space as a Context for Learning About Self and Other

Infants' social play with peers begins simply—an infant offering a book to another infant, or a shake of the head and a laugh while watching another infant shake her head and smile. This early play grows into shared imitation of familiar experiences. For example, one infant holds an empty cup near another infant, who pretends to drink from the cup. Such peer play emerges spontaneously.

A month into the new school year, Vicki and Jodie, coteachers at a cooperative preschool, notice how 13-month-old Etta and 14-month-old Elena often play alongside each other, each pursuing her own play but doing so near the other. One hides behind a curtain, and within minutes, the other follows. If one goes to the other side of the yard, within minutes, so does the other. The teachers also witness and capture in photos two younger infants, Emilio and Greta, as they share a mutual interest and curiosity. Emilio shakes a metal spice tin while Greta watches. Soon, Emilio reaches toward Greta, spice tin in hand, and waits. After a pause, Greta takes it and shakes it up and down. Emilio watches, reaches toward Greta, waits, but Greta continues to shake the tin up and down. Reaching to her with open palm, Emilio looks intently at Greta,

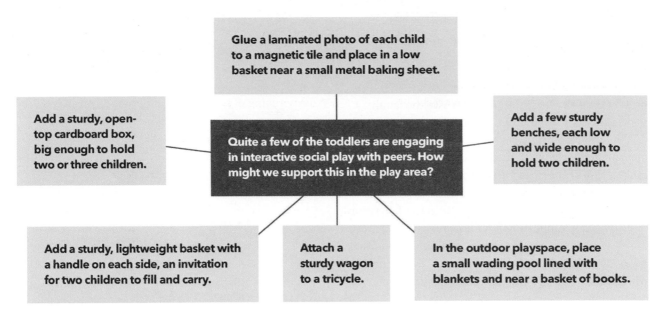

Planning web: Places to be together

but then he spies a feather on the ground, picks it up, holds it out toward Greta, and waits, watching her expectantly.

Were the teachers witnessing the blossoming of friendships? Although playing independently, each child remained aware of what the other was doing. With Emilio and Greta, there appeared to be an experiment in give and take, a first encounter with sharing, a simple negotiation.

These observations and interpretations prompted this question, "What might we add to the infants' play space to support emerging friendships with peers?" Ideas that emerged were recorded on a *planning web*. A planning web is a simple way to hold possible ideas for what teachers might offer (see "Planning Web: Places to Be Together"). By sifting through the proposed ideas, teachers can decide what to offer next in support of infants' learning.

After exploring several ideas of what they might add to the play space to support peer play, teachers Vicki and Jodie added a sturdy, wide cardboard box of sufficient size to hold two or three children. Outdoors, they converted a small pool into a place to share books. With these additions to the play space, they watched to see what the infants did in response.

This illustrates a reflective planning cycle that begins with observing and then continues as teachers document and interpret significant moments (California Department of Education 2016;

Maguire-Fong 2020). (See "Reflective Planning Cycle" on page 66.) When teachers share with others what they document, and when they interpret together its meaning, they generate ideas for what context to offer next to support infants in going deeper in their explorations (Maguire-Fong 2020). Once teachers prepare and offer a new context, the cycle begins anew—observing, documenting, and interpreting to guide curriculum and to identify emerging skills and concepts.

Daily Routines as a Context for Learning

The reflective planning cycle also supports teachers in designing routines as contexts for learning. Infants and toddlers in early learning settings experience a series of routines that mark their day, and each routine is a context for learning about self and other. The first daily routine is the baby's arrival, coupled with the family member's departure. It is helpful to plan with the family a departure ritual that can be repeated each day and that gives infants an opportunity to actively participate. To begin, a teacher might acknowledge how the departure feels to the parent and to the baby, saying, for example: "It's hard to think about your baby being upset when you leave. Babies are often sad when they see their parents leave. Let's explore how we might help your baby learn to make sense of your leaving. Over time, she'll come to associate the sadness of seeing you leave with the joy that comes when you return."

The goal is to acknowledge a family's desire to protect the baby from sadness, to invite the family to consider how their child is trying to make sense of this emotionally trying experience, and to brainstorm ideas with the family that respect infants' attempts to make sense of the departure. "Planning Web: Ideas to Help with Separation," on page 67, illustrates how teachers Vicki and Jodie used a planning web to record their ideas for supporting families whose infants were upset when the parent departed. "Plan of Possibilities: A Goodbye Ritual," below, documents what occurred when the teachers planned a goodbye ritual with one of the families.

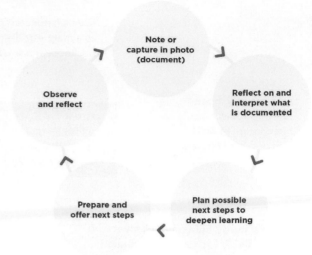

Reflective planning cycle

Plan of Possibilities: A Goodbye Ritual

Context: We are creating goodbye rituals with the infants' families. One is that the departing family member gestures and says goodbye as the infant watches. We also collect laminated family photos and place them in a basket near the entry.

Planning question: How will the infants respond to a predictable goodbye ritual?

Observation: Twelve-month-old Etta trails her father to the door as he prepares to leave. She looks up at him. He smiles at her and waves, saying, "Goodbye, Etta. I'll be back." Etta drops to the floor and begins to cry. Her father squats near her and lifts her chin so that she looks up at him. He touches his fingers to his lips and throws her a kiss. He again says, "Goodbye. I'll be back. I am going to work." She watches him leave and continues to cry. Then she turns and crawls toward me. I help her find the photo of her family from the family photo basket. She clutches the photo and gazes at it.

Interpretation: Although Etta was sad during this new goodbye ritual, she remained involved and active. As soon as her father was out of sight, Etta crawled toward me, her primary care teacher. Her cries softened by the time she reached me. Looking at the photo of her family seemed to calm her. If we repeat this each day, I think she will have a surety that her father has departed. Also, she will begin to associate the phrase "Goodbye. I'll be back" with "Hello! I came back!"

Conversations and Interactions as a Context for Learning About Self and Other

A third context for learning are the many conversations and interactions that infants and toddlers have with adults throughout the day. What distinguishes this from the other two contexts—play space and routines—is that the focus in planning is on what the teacher intentionally says or does to support children's understanding. To thoughtfully propose possibilities for talking and interacting with infants and toddlers in ways that support social and emotional growth, teachers can adopt the approach of a researcher by listening and observing to discover what children reveal through actions, gestures, or vocalizations.

DAP Observing, listening, and responding with sensitivity make children feel psychologically safe and welcomed. Teachers make sure that each child hears and sees their home language, culture, family, and social identity affirmed in positive ways.

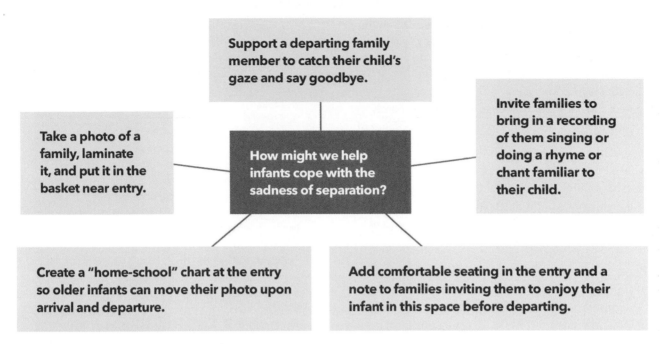

Support a departing family member to catch their child's gaze and say goodbye.

Take a photo of a family, laminate it, and put it in the basket near entry.

How might we help infants cope with the sadness of separation?

Invite families to bring in a recording of them singing or doing a rhyme or chant familiar to their child.

Create a "home-school" chart at the entry so older infants can move their photo upon arrival and departure.

Add comfortable seating in the entry and a note to families inviting them to enjoy their infant in this space before departing.

Planning web: Ideas to help with separation

Carol, a teacher at a college children's center, documented this interaction as she observed toddlers at play:

> Nate, 25 months old, draws on a paper, and I say, "I see you are making marks on the paper."
>
> "Lola," he responds.
>
> "Oh, you are drawing Lola!" I remark.
>
> He looks at me and repeats, "Lola." I give him a new piece of paper, on which he makes small marks, all the while repeating, "Lola."
>
> "You are drawing Lola this time too, aren't you?" I say.
>
> Nate's smile grows wider, and he sings, "Lola, Lola, Lola," before saying, "Eyes, ears."
>
> "Oh, those are Lola's eyes and ears," I reply.
>
> He makes more marks and says, "Lola, me."
>
> "And that's you, Nate," I say.
>
> At pickup time, I show Nate's mother the drawing. She explains that "Lola" is what Nate calls his grandmother, who has recently departed on a trip. She adds that Nate is very close to his grandmother.

Nate's markings were more than just scribbles—they revealed his thoughts and feelings. Nate expressed through his marks his story of missing Lola. After reviewing her documentation of her interaction with Nate and her conversation with his mother, Carol and her coteachers decided to listen more closely whenever the older infants explored the writing tools. They wanted to listen for other examples of children revealing feelings or thoughts as they draw.

This vignette illustrates how very young children communicate feelings and thoughts through one-word responses, gestures, facial expressions, and actions. Documentation, when shared and interpreted together with coworkers and children's families, generates ideas for what to offer next to support children in making sense of what may feel like confusing and troubling feelings. In other situations, not uncommon in infant care, those feelings might lead to actions that cross the boundaries of acceptable behavior. Infants and toddlers may bite or hit others, resist trusted caregivers' requests, or erupt in tantrums. At times, such behavior is sparked by curiosity, and at other times, it is fueled by feelings of anger or frustration. This is not unlike the frustration a lost traveler might feel in an unfamiliar country, surrounded by an unfamiliar language. In each situation, a trusted guide can provide helpful support in making sense of what to do, how to do it, or where to go next.

> A crawler approaches another crawler and, with a look of curiosity, tugs on this child's hair, causing the child to cry. A nearby teacher sees this,

approaches quickly, and says to the crying child, "Ooh, that hurt," while simultaneously touching both of the children's hair, and then saying: "Gently, no pulling hair. Pulling hair hurts. Gentle touches, not rough."

With older infants and toddlers, a conflict might arise when two children want the same toy. "Plan of Possibilities: Using Clear Limits and Redirection," below, illustrates how a group of teachers proposed a plan of possibilities designed to support older infants in figuring out what it means to have and to give, and in time, to build understanding of the concept of sharing.

When conflicts arise, infants and toddlers struggle to cope with intense feelings, and they rely on the thoughtful words and actions of a caring adult to help them hold and contain strong feelings, while simultaneously resolving a distressing situation (Maguire-Fong & Peralta 2018). With thoughtful words and actions, teachers acknowledge strong feelings or desires, clearly describe what children may not do and why, and clearly describe what they may do instead (Maguire-Fong 2020).

Rather than seeing misbehavior as simply a disruption to end and move beyond, it helps to see it as a context for learning that deserves thoughtful planning.

Plan of Possibilities: Using Clear Limits and Redirection

Context: Among the older infants, we have noticed more frequent conflicts over possession of a desired object.

Planning question: How will the children respond when we clearly acknowledge their feelings, intention, or desire; describe what they did that was not acceptable and why; and clearly state what is acceptable the next time this situation arises?

Observation: I see Jackson hold tightly to the handlebar of a trike as Linnea attempts to push him off the trike. I approach, kneel between them, and say, "Linnea, I will not let you push Jackson off the trike. I can see that you are angry and that you really want the trike, but Jackson is still using it. You can ask him, 'Please, may I use the trike?'" I watch and wait. Linnea frowns and silently looks

down. I say to Jackson, "Linnea wants to use the trike too, so when you are through, you can give it to her." Linnea, still frowning, looks at Jackson and says, "My trike," but she does not attempt to grab the trike.

Interpretation: Linnea wants the trike and is dismayed because Jackson has it. Because she sees him as the one keeping her from the trike, I understand why she tries to push him off the trike. After all, he is the obstacle keeping her from the trike. I also understand her anger, but I cannot let her push him off the trike. I acknowledge her anger, but in the same breath I tell her that she may not push him off the trike. I want her to learn that pushing others in hurtful ways is not acceptable. Because I also want her to know what to do the next time she finds herself in this situation, I give her a phrase to use to request the trike. In her own way, she asks Jackson for the trike and resists pushing him.

When teachers listen well to the stories that infants and toddlers tell through actions, gestures, and expressions and when teachers hold these stories in mind by documenting, sharing, and interpreting them together, they find ways to help infants and toddlers master the challenge and experience the joy of making and keeping friends. In short, when observant and reflective teachers plan thoughtful play spaces, daily routines, and conversations and interactions as contexts for learning, they help infants and toddlers find answers to these questions: "Where's my family?" and "Who's my friend?"

MARY JANE MAGUIRE-FONG, MS, is professor emerita at American River College, a former teacher and administrator for birth to age 5 programs serving migrant farmworker families, and an author.

PART 4

Teaching to Enhance Each Child's Development and Learning

The 2-year-olds come in from outdoors and hang up their coats. Mr. William, their teacher, has baskets of books and fine motor activities waiting. Javon picks out *Me and My Mama: Celebrate Black Joy and Family Love*, by Carole Boston Weatherford, from a basket. He sits on Mr. William's lap, and Miya and Remy sit on one side. Mr. William points to the pictures and asks, "Oh, look. Do you play with your mama on the floor?" and "Do you make a fort with chairs and a blanket?" Miya points to the picture and says, "That's me." "Yes, Miya, that looks just like you reading with your mama," smiles Mr. William. "That's me," says Javon. "Do you make a big fort with your brother Booker?" "Big fort," says Javon.

Warm, responsive relationships provide the essential starting point for infants' and toddlers' learning and development. In the company of caring adults, children playfully explore, discover, and try new skills. Playful connections take place during one-on-one interactions, as teachers are attuned to children's verbal and nonverbal cues and needs. During feeding and mealtime, care routines, play, and personal conversations, children develop a sense of identity with the people and experiences around them. Educators notice the ways children play, join in their laughter during funny moments, and celebrate their new skills and accomplishments.

While educators understand the needs of the group as a whole, developmentally appropriate teaching with infants and toddlers is individualized and child centered. Educators recognize and follow the curiosity and choices of each child, adjusting materials and levels of support to encourage their confidence. They know children enjoy repeating tasks and that this is important for them to master new skills. Teachers remember favorite activities, stories, songs, and games that delight and encourage joyful self-expression.

Infants and toddlers develop their identity in the context of their families, languages, cultures, and neighborhood experiences. Because development is anchored in the cultural contexts of families, all learning experiences are planned and carried out in ways that are developmentally, linguistically, and culturally responsive. Educators follow predictable schedules and routines so children feel confident about what will happen and how adults will respond. This consistency creates a safe, secure space for learning.

Educators understand that children develop at their own pace. Building on each child's unique interests, knowledge, and skills, teachers adjust supports to meet children's needs, including dual language learners, children with delays and disabilities, and children whose learning is advanced. They notice children's needs for active and quiet play and also protect solitary play. They respond to children's current and emerging skills by offering a range of challenges and sensory experiences. When children play near each other, educators help them notice what others are doing and express their needs.

Many teaching strategies support joyful learning for infants and toddlers, and just like selecting the appropriate tool from a toolbox, you select materials, activities, and other elements that are suited to the specific situation and characteristics of the children. Educators remain attuned to children's attention level, signs of fatigue, and response to stimulation, and they ensure that children receive the appropriate level of support.

To meet these goals, educators coordinate responsibilities and tasks with colleagues. They develop a deep knowledge of each child and family and use their understandings and insights to nurture and encourage children's learning and to celebrate each child's accomplishments.

In Part 4, you will encounter stories and examples that show how developmentally appropriate practices ensure joyful, meaningful learning experiences for infants and toddlers.

READ AND REFLECT

As you read the chapters in this section, consider and evaluate your own classroom practices using these reflection questions.

"What to Teach Before Talking: Developing Communication Skills Across Home and Early Learning Contexts" encourages collaboration with families to support children's early expressive skills, vocalizations, and gestures through systematic strategies that promote language during daily routines and activities. **Consider:** How can you become more purposeful in noticing and documenting children's attempts to communicate? What targeted skills can you use to encourage children's emerging language and communication?

"The Power of Pause: Moments of Silence and Early Emotional and Language Development" highlights the benefits of silent moments to support emotional connection and language development in infants and toddlers. It explains the power of pausing, as teachers become attuned to children's experiences. **Consider:** What emotional experiences do you notice in yourself as you are working with children? Do you find you need to quiet your own thoughts and refocus your attention on individual children? How do children respond when you practice attunement during moments of silence?

"Strengthening Infant and Toddler Teaching with Explicit Language Skills" presents the positive impact of designing teaching in response to each child's unique ways of engaging and learning. The authors share effective strategies to promote concept development, language, and cognitive skills. **Consider:** What might distract you from engaging with children in personal conversations? How can you structure your schedule to make explicit language interactions a priority?

"'You're Okay' May Not Be Okay: Using Emotion Language to Promote Toddlers' Social and Emotional Development" offers strategies, examples, and activities to help you support toddlers' social and emotional development using emotion language. It encourages self-reflection and anti-bias, anti-oppressive approaches to social and emotional teaching. **Consider:** What

emotions exhibited by children make you realize a need to be more patient, self-reflect, and evaluate your bias? How do cultural norms influence the way you feel about children's expression of emotion?

"We Put Paper on the Floor: Supporting the Emergent Literacy Skills of Infants and Toddlers" invites you to consider children's wonder and excitement as they discover self-expression, creativity, and joy in early literacy development. It suggests steps and processes to include families and enhance children's first writing experiences. **Consider:** How do literacy activities for infants and toddlers differ from those of older children? Are children in your program able to select other activities and return to a literacy project when they are ready? What new literacy experiences would you like to try?

NEXT STEPS

After reading Part 4, consider the following suggestions as you plan next steps in making learning individualized, engaging, and appropriately challenging for each child.

1. Identify the teaching strategies you currently use that incorporate the contexts of the children and families. What strategies can you add to make play spaces, routines, and activities more fully reflect children's multiple diversities and responsive to children's individual ways of learning?

2. What steps can you take to coordinate with families and colleagues to support children in more culturally congruent ways during caring routines and transitions?

3. How are play experiences prepared to address the learning and development of the group while offering individualized teaching for each child? What strategies can you use to identify and support specific learning goals for each area of development?

References for the chapters in this part can be accessed online at NAEYC.org/books/focus-infants-toddlers.

CHAPTER 14

What to Teach Before Talking
Developing Communication Skills Across Home and Early Learning Contexts

Mollie Romano, Jennifer A. Brown, Christan Coogle, Jennifer R. Ottley, and Emily M. Rose

Tasha is an experienced teacher in a toddler room in a community-based early learning program. Camila, an 18-month-old girl, joined her class a few months ago. Camila's mother, Veronica, is concerned that Camila does not communicate much and wonders if it could be because she is exposed to two languages. Veronica's parents are Puerto Rican, and Veronica and Camila were both born in the continental United States. While the program staff and Camila's parents primarily communicate in English, Camila hears Spanish from her grandparents, who are important home caregivers for Camila, and in her community. Tasha reassures Veronica that being bilingual is an asset for children and that it will not negatively impact Camila's early communication development. However, like monolingual children, children learning two languages might show signs of an early delay that are unrelated to dual language learning.

On Tasha's suggestion, Veronica completes a questionnaire that is part of a developmental screening. Tasha notes that the screener indicates a need for further evaluation and helps Veronica connect with the local agency that offers this service. Tasha suggests that they can add communication supports throughout Camila's day at home and at the center. While Veronica and Tasha agree that they would like to see Camila begin to use a few words in both languages, Tasha shares that there are many communication skills that lead up to learning words that they could help Camila to build on.

Knowing how early communication skills build on one another and how each skill contributes to a child's language development can assist teachers and families as they support children in the earliest years. While adults are often eager for children to use words, beginning with foundational language skills—including

vocalizations, shared (or joint) attention, and gestures—aids children's progress toward speaking. In this chapter, we outline the development of these skills and share ways teachers and families can support children to develop them.

Early Expressive Skills

Early childhood educators rely on their understanding of child development to effectively support each and every child in their settings. While each child has unique assets and characteristics due to their cultural context, lived experiences, and individual differences, general progressions of development can be identified and used to guide the choice of targeted skills and strategies.

During the first year of life, children begin to make sense of the speech sounds around them, gain more motor control to make speech sounds, and communicate their own wants and needs by using gestures. Infants also make significant strides in social skills and interactions as they learn that they can communicate for several purposes or functions and that others who communicate with them have different perspectives from their own. Vocalizations, shared (or joint) attention, and gestures are expressive skills that can serve as a starting place for fostering communication development in children who are learning one language, children who are multilingual, or children with disabilities—even before they begin to use words.

Vocalizations

When babies are born, they communicate primarily through their cries. An infant's cries differ depending on the message the baby needs to send, signaling

hunger, pain, or even boredom. Cries do not require much motor control from a baby's tongue and lips, or articulators (Stoel-Gammon 1998), as speech sounds do.

As babies reach 2 to 3 months of age, they often develop well-defined vowel sounds and early consonant sounds like /k/ and /g/ that are made at the back of the mouth (Stoel-Gammon 1998). Then, around 6 to 7 months, babies start to use more sounds, like /p/ and /b/ (Gros-Louis & Miller 2018). In the second half of their first year, they produce sounds in strings of babbles, starting with repeated sounds like "babababab" or "mamamama." During this phase, babies begin to produce a wider variety of consonants and even play with nonspeech sounds like raspberries (Stoel-Gammon 1998). Later in their first year, most babies begin to babble or vocalize with different strings of sounds like "bagadama." Babies are gaining more and more control of their articulators to make these sound combinations.

Having speech sounds in their "babble vocabularies" is important so that as infants come to understand the label and meaning of words and actions, they can form the sounds into words. Vocalizations are also important in the development of social interactions. Infants learn that they can engage in back-and-forth exchanges (early conversations) with others by using sounds (Stoel-Gammon 1998). Infants who vocalize more often go on to develop stronger communication skills (Morgan et al. 2020), so supporting the use of speech sounds could help children progress toward word use.

Shared, or Joint, Attention

Shared attention, also called *joint attention,* occurs when an infant shifts their gaze or focus between an object or event of interest and another person to include that person in the moment (Bakeman & Adamson 1984). Shared attention is a social communication skill. It indicates a baby's understanding that each person has their own perspective and that the baby can secure another person's attention to refer to an object or event so that they are sharing in it together (Adamson & Chance 1998). For example, a child may point to a bird outside, and their sibling may look at it and comment, "That's a blue jay! It found the birdfeeder." The baby initiated joint attention by pointing and looking at their sibling. Shared attention skills are important because they help a child determine what others are paying attention to, and they provide a clue into the meaning of the words other people are using (Adamson & Chance 1998).

Infants are not born with the ability to share attention with others, but they develop it over time, and it is a critical skill for social interaction and communication competence. Children progress from attending to the faces of their caregivers in early infancy to following the adult's shifting focus to an object or action of interest, which involves responding to joint attention. Later, infants learn to initiate joint attention by drawing a caregiver's attention to their own object or action of interest with their gaze and with gestures.

Lauren Adamson and her colleagues (2019) found that children who spend less time engaging in shared attention often have lower vocabulary knowledge than those who have strengths in joint or shared attention. Their study examined the role of autism spectrum disorder (ASD) and its influence on joint attention and language skills for children with and without ASD. Children with ASD may struggle to develop shared attention skills, which may then impact word learning (Adamson et al. 2019).

Gestures

Gestures typically emerge within the context of shared attention (Crais, Watson, & Baranek 2009). For example, when Camila touches a picture of a train in her book, she is using a gesture to express the message "Look, Ms. Tasha." Early gestures include contact gestures, such as touching an object (contact pointing), giving an object to another person, and pushing something away (Morgan et al. 2020). Next, children use distal gestures that refer to something farther away, such as pointing toward an object and reaching. Both contact and distal gestures are context dependent—pointing toward a banana in the kitchen likely means a child is requesting the banana. Later in the day, when the child points out the window at a dog running by the house, they are likely commenting on and showing their communication partner the neighbor's fast-moving pet. A child's early use of gestures serves as a bridge to language use; typically, words for objects that children point to enter their

vocabularies in subsequent months (Kishimoto 2017). Pointing, especially, has been linked to vocabulary development in infants and toddlers. The more children point, the more words they begin to use (Colonnesi et al. 2010).

Representational gestures develop later, and each has a specific meaning (Crais, Watson, & Baranek 2009). For example, when a toddler holds their fists up and turns them to represent a steering wheel, they are communicating a message about a car, whether they are in the kitchen wondering where their toy car is or looking out the window and commenting on the neighbor's car on the street. Gestures are good communication skills to target before children start to speak because they often serve as a bridge to symbolic language, in part by eliciting specific responses from caregivers. Research shows that adults are more likely to respond verbally to a gesture than to vocalization (Kishimoto 2017; Wu & Gros-Louis 2014), perhaps because the communicative intent behind the gesture is clear. This is important because as a child learns to gesture, they are able to seek language input from others. Helping a child learn more types of gestures enables them to communicate a clear message.

During the meeting with Veronica, Tasha uses a handout from the First Words Project (n.d.) to share an overview of early expressive communication milestones with Veronica, highlighting the steps that happen before children typically produce spoken words. Veronica knew that children babbled before using words, but she had not thought about gestures and shared attention as being important communication steps before children use words. (Visit NAEYC.org/books/focus-infants-toddlers to see an overview of early expressive communication targets.)

Veronica notes that pointing stands out to her as a good focus. Camila will occasionally point, but she is not yet consistently pointing to show what she is interested in or to request something. Tasha agrees, mentioning how and why pointing is important for children as they grow. She offers to share a few resources with Veronica about pointing. Pointing will also help Camila establish shared attention with other adults and children. Tasha adds that increasing Camila's pointing might also help her become less frustrated at the center and at home because she will be better able to communicate her intent to others.

Identifying Strategies to Promote Early Expressive Communication

After Tasha and Veronica identified pointing gestures as an early expressive communication target for Camila, they considered ways to support her use of the gestures at home and at the center. Choosing strategies helps teachers and families be more intentional in supporting the child's early communication target, both at home and in the early learning setting. In this case, there are several strategies that Tasha and Veronica could choose from to support Camila's pointing gestures. (See NAEYC.org/books/focus-infants-toddlers to see examples of what Camila's family and teacher can look for and support in both the home and program contexts.)

One important strategy for supporting infant pointing is to model pointing with words (Romano, Eugenio, & Kiratzis 2021; Rowe & Leech 2019). Research shows that babies who have caregivers who point more also point more themselves months later (e.g., Kishimoto 2017). While many teachers and families think about modeling language during their interactions with infants and toddlers, they may not think about modeling gestures too.

A second strategy to support a child's use of pointing gestures is environmental arrangement—including highly preferred materials during play and placing desired objects where the child can see them but cannot reach them (Kaiser, Hancock, & Nietfeld 2000; Kaiser & Roberts 2013). Environmental arrangements (putting objects in sight but out of reach, holding up an object and waiting, or offering choices) have been effectively used in many models of early communication intervention for children with language learning delays and disabilities (Fey et al. 2006; Kaiser, Hancock, & Nietfeld 2000). This creates an opportunity for the child to use gestures to communicate for desired items. For some infants, this strategy might increase the likelihood that they will point, especially to request the desired object.

Tasha and Veronica talk about several strategies for helping Camila point, but they settle on two primary strategies: modeling gestures with words and environmental arrangements. Veronica thinks that modeling gestures will take some practice for her to get used to, but it will tap into the assets of Marco (Camila's dad) and Camila's abuelita (Lita)—they actively use their hands while talking already. Veronica thinks they will have an easy time remembering to do it if they remind themselves that it helps clarify what their words mean. Lita and Marco will focus on modeling pointing while using single words in Spanish to help build Camila's vocabulary. Tasha says that she will also model gestures and use short phrases in English when they look at books together and when they pass by the classroom door that is decorated with new pictures each month.

Tasha asks about desired objects that they could use in environmental arrangements that Camila might point to in order to get them. Veronica suggests that Camila may be motivated to point to get her stuffed bunny, Hops, before naptime at the center. Tasha plans to put the bunny on a shelf to prompt Camila to point. She adds that they may also need to plan for what to do if Camila gets upset and does not quite know how to get Hops yet. Tasha and Veronica keep problem-solving, and they conclude that modeling a point and saying, "You want Hops!" might be a good way to help Camila learn what to do to get him down from the shelf.

Choosing Daily Routines to Implement New Strategies and Support Skills

Infants and toddlers learn within the context of everyday routines and activities in early learning settings and at home. Everyday routines support children's learning because they are predictable, are repeatable, and have a role for the child built into them (Spagnola & Fiese 2007; Woods, Kashinath, & Goldstein 2004). A key feature of language support is to choose specific routines for integrating strategies to help the child begin to use their targeted skill. Some routines might have more opportunities for a certain target skill and may lend themselves more naturally to certain strategies. Thinking about the fit between the routine, the target skill, and the strategy can help teachers make decisions about their instructional plan. The goal is to increase opportunities for the child;

identifying and planning for a few additional contexts and partners can encourage a child to use their skills in meaningful ways.

Tasha and Veronica focus on high-impact moments that happen naturally throughout the course of the day. They choose routines at home and at the program, then fill out a chart with what they would like to see Camila do in each routine (point), who has what role, and which strategies they will use to support her. (You can see more of this process along with the chart at NAEYC.org/books/focus-infants-toddlers.)

DAP Tasha strategically uses Camila's language and cultural ways of learning to enhance her communication, expression, and learning. She sets clearly defined educational goals that reflect the family's input as well as Camila's own background knowledge and experiences. Importantly, she fully aligns Camila's learning in the program setting with the family's equally important contributions at home.

Conclusion

Tasha, Veronica, and other members of Camila's family have jointly developed a plan to support Camila's early communication in two languages while she awaits further evaluation through a local program. Identifying key expressive language targets, instructional strategies, and routine contexts for learning promotes children's communication development by building on their current skills during everyday interactions. Once Camila's teacher and family begin to use their plan, they can keep track of whether they are implementing their strategies in routines and how it is going for Camila. With partnerships between early childhood educators and families and systematic planning, children like Camila can develop into expressive communicators.

CHRISTAN COOGLE, PhD, BCBA, LBA, is an associate professor of early childhood special education at George Mason University in Fairfax, Virginia.

JENNIFER R. OTTLEY, PhD, is research director of the Systems Development & Improvement Center at the University of Cincinnati.

EMILY M. ROSE, PhD, is a clinical assistant professor in the Department of Rehabilitation Sciences in the Beaver College of Health Sciences at Appalachian State University. She is a speech-language pathologist specializing in pediatric language disorders.

MOLLIE ROMANO, PhD, CCC-SLP, is an associate professor in the School of Communication Science and Disorders at Florida State University.

JENNIFER A. BROWN, PhD, CCC-SLP, is an associate professor and graduate coordinator in the Department of Communication Sciences and Special Education at the University of Georgia in Athens.

CHAPTER 15

The Power of Pause
Moments of Silence and Early Emotional and Language Development

Nodelyn Abayan

During my 22 years in the field of early childhood education, I've noted the benefits of silent moments to support both emotional and language development in infants and toddlers. In this chapter, I explain more about the connection between teachers incorporating moments of silence and children's development in these areas. I offer several strategies you can use to embrace these moments of silence in your interactions with young children and to reflect on that practice.

Intentional Silence to Support Emotional Development

For 15 years, I mentored undergraduate and graduate interns, who were pursuing a degree in child development, in a laboratory school setting. One intern, Sheerin, asked for my help with an inconsolable 8-month-old baby. Sheerin was frantic and tried everything she could think of to help the child—putting her down for a nap, changing her diaper, and feeding her. Still, the child wept. I calmly approached Sheerin while she, the other interns, and the children were all sitting on the floor. I told her, "Just be with her in her distress. If you assure her that you are there for her with your calm presence, you do not need to say a word. It will be all right." Sheerin did exactly that, and slowly but surely the baby calmed down.

To process our thoughts, we need silence. We tend to focus better in a quieter environment, and silence helps restore our finite cognitive resources. Indeed, "silence is crucial for the mind to register information from its surroundings; thus, it is inactivity, generally in silence, that stimulates brain activity most" (Brown 2019, 28). In an age that seems filled with loud sounds and distracting noises, silence is essential.

We often underestimate the power of our silent presence to help us form a deep connection with a child. An adult's intentional silence is an intervention strategy during a child's emotionally loaded moments of distress, helping them to learn the language of co-regulation (Tavares 2022). I've come to think of this as "loving silence." Loving silence speaks to what is underneath the behavior and creates space and time for seemingly uncomfortable emotions to be honored, attended to, and recognized. While it's easy to write about this strategy, it can be very difficult to put into practice. Yet young children depend on intentional teachers to guide them in learning about and navigating their emotions.

Pausing to Support Language Development

In my work with infants, I have seen the power of pausing. Pausing gives time for a baby to process the sounds of the words they hear and to respond in the way they want to respond. Infants' brains are just beginning to understand the various sounds needed to form words. This typically includes the pitch of our voice (Kuhl 2004), which usually goes up when we ask a question. Too often, babies are not given time to process what they've just heard before more questions are asked of them. By frequently pausing, an educator can give an infant or toddler time to vocalize. This can turn into an alternating exchange between them—where both are active participants. An infant's active participation in vocal exchanges, together with adult language input (Soderstrom 2007), lays the basis for child speech and conversational development (Golinkoff et al. 2015; Oller et al. 2019). Reading books, narrating what you are doing, and singing rhymes and songs are all crucial for early language learning and development, but pausing and silence are important too. I've learned that if I pause, infants and toddlers respond.

To try this out, ask an infant one question, then look them in the eyes and pause (try counting silently to three to remind yourself to pause). In my experience, most babies respond when there is a bit of a pause. They smile, coo, say "ahh," or babble. As an extension of this, think about words and phrases that they hear over and over, which invites very young children to notice patterns in sounds. For example, infants can start to notice patterns in the sounds of familiar songs (Holliday, n.d.). Try leaving out the last word of a favorite song. You may be surprised that infants and toddlers can finish it for you. A pause helps them begin to experiment with sounds and even words. When we include silent pauses in talking (and singing) with infants and toddlers, it helps support their early language learning and development.

The Importance of Reflection

Part of respectful and responsive infant and toddler education is providing the time and space for them to respond. This takes patience and practice on the part of the early childhood educator. Reflecting on your practice can help us understand and appreciate the role of silence in young children's development.

DAP Listening and seeking to understand what children may be trying to communicate provide a starting point for reflective practice. By learning from children, teachers recognize and build on their multiple assets and strengths.

As a mentor, I have taught interns how to journal their interactions with infants and do careful observations of others' turn-taking interactions with infants. Journaling and observing are important skills for early educators. They can enhance our practice and deepen our understanding of why we do what we do and how we might improve our practices. Reflection is integral to intentional, effective teaching.

To try this out, notice what happens when you pause: before forming another sentence during an interaction with a baby, what do you observe about the infant and about yourself? What effect does pausing have?

You may find that the power of pause affects you too.

NODELYN ABAYAN, EdD, received her doctorate in Educational Leadership and Social Justice at San Francisco State University. She has been an infant and toddler head teacher, mentor, coach, education manager, and adjunct professor and is currently an instructor in Child and Family Studies at City College of San Francisco.

CHAPTER 16

Strengthening Infant and Toddler Teaching with Explicit Language Skills

Allyson Dean and Linda Groves Gillespie

Take 1

Sonya is reading a story to 18-month-old Todd. Todd points to a picture of a horse and says, "Dog." Sonya says, "That's a horse." Todd says, "Horse." "Right," says Sonya and then turns the page.

Take 2

Sonya is reading a story to 18-month-old Todd. Todd points to a picture of a horse and says, "Dog." Sonya says, "I can see why you think it's a dog. It has four legs, pointy ears, and a tail. But let's look closer. This animal is much bigger than a dog and look, this part of its face, the muzzle, is much longer than a dog's." She points to the nose as Todd watches intently. Sonya says, "This animal is called a horse. Let's look for a picture of a dog." She flips through the book and finds a picture of a dog. "See, here's a dog. It's much smaller than a horse. Let's look at them together." She folds the page so Todd can see the pictures side by side, allowing time for him to look at both pictures. As Todd points again, Sonya says, "Yes, here's the horse and here's the dog—they look different. The horse is much bigger, his legs are longer, and he has a longer muzzle, which is another word for nose." Sonya pauses again while Todd points to the animals. She names them as he points. Then she says, "The horse and the dog are both animals, but they are different types of animals."

The act of teaching is defined as "activities that impart knowledge or skill" (www.vocabulary.com/dictionary/teaching). Babies learn from their environment and the people in it, so it's important for teachers to feel confident that the knowledge and skills they are teaching are developmentally appropriate for the age of the children in their groups. This learning often happens through everyday interactions such as the scenario above. The teacher expands Todd's knowledge

of animals by acting on both Todd's interest in labeling and his developmental readiness to discriminate differences between a horse and a dog.

Direct Teaching

Good teaching practices expand children's understanding of concepts by offering new information and extending learning opportunities in ways that fit with each child's unique understanding, strengths, and cultural and linguistic contexts. One of the teaching practices in the above scenario is called *direct* or *explicit* teaching, in which teachers use intentional strategies to give children specific information, define words, and link ideas to children's experiences (Lorio & Woods 2020). This interaction builds or bridges children's knowledge in a particular area of cognitive development—in Todd's case, categorizing animals. Teachers expand children's learning during everyday experiences as they watch for opportunities to clarify and build on babies' and toddlers' current knowledge and understanding. In reality, both of the above scenarios are examples of direct or explicit teaching, but the quality of that teaching practice varies considerably from the first to the second interaction.

In the first scenario, Sonya tells Todd the correct word for the animal, elicits a rote response from him, and quickly moves on. This exchange offers Todd some new information—a new vocabulary word, perhaps—but doesn't build on his knowledge of dogs or clarify that the horse is actually a different type of animal than a dog. He may offer the word *horse* the next time he looks at this book with his teacher, but most likely, Todd does not understand why one animal picture is labeled a *horse* and the other a *dog*. In short, he did not develop an expanded understanding of these two animals and what makes them different.

Building New Knowledge

In the second scenario, Sonya uses Todd's understanding of dogs to help him build new knowledge about horses. By offering explicit information about the similarities and differences in the two types of animals, Sonya helps Todd to extend his understanding of the terms *horse* and *dog* and begin to understand that there are many types of creatures that make up the category "animals." She also helps him begin to develop a mental picture of the two animals by pointing out visual differences between them. Finally, Sonya provides Todd with a strategy for differentiating animals. By pointing out the differences aloud, she models the process for Todd, and he can begin to tell these animals apart by their individual attributes such as size and type of nose. She is skillfully connecting what he knows to what he doesn't quite yet know.

Sonya's interaction with Todd in the second scenario offers teaching that extends beyond the domain of cognitive development. That's an exciting part of teaching with infants and toddlers—areas of development are interconnected (The Urban Child Institute, n.d.). Because infants' and toddlers' development is holistic—that is to say, growth in one developmental area boosts growth in another—effective teaching practices also take a holistic approach (Dolev, Sher-Censor, & Tai 2021). This requires teachers to understand the knowledge and skills in each developmental domain for each child and to address these in their teaching.

So what other developmental skills or knowledge does the interaction above help Todd acquire? First, Sonya responds to Todd's label of *dog*. This action is teaching Todd that he is worthy of attention and cared about, and that his thoughts and contributions are important, which builds his sense of self-confidence and his understanding of a friendship—part of the social and emotional domain. Then Sonya responds to Todd's language by describing the illustration and offering a new word to describe the animal in the picture: *horse*. This new language builds on Todd's attempt to label the animal in the picture. As Sonya offers information and then pauses for a response from Todd (verbal or nonverbal), Todd is beginning to understand the rules of conversation. He also knows that Sonya will wait for him and follow his lead in this back-and forth interaction.

Conversations like this one, where teachers offer new or different information to children and then pause to watch and listen for a response, assist children like Todd in acquiring a rich and complex vocabulary. Such conversations also offer children experience with the pragmatics of conversation—the back-and-forth flow of communication and how specific social contexts contribute to making meaning, such as gestures, turn taking, or focusing interest on an activity (Muhinyi & Rowe 2019). Note that this type of interaction is no accident: Sonya has a deep understanding about infant and toddler development, gained through years of experience and education and ongoing reflection and learning, that informs her practice. She documents what she observes in Todd's behavior and play throughout the day and uses those observations to inform and shape her practice. That's what makes Sonya a good teacher.

In infant and toddler settings, effective teaching practices and instructional strategies look very different from those used with older children, but they still reflect teachers' use of thoughtful, intentional interactions and activities to engage young children. These interactions reflect the teachers' unique relationship with each child in their care and build on their knowledge and observation of each child's development, allowing them to take advantage of learning opportunities that emerge through daily routines.

EQUITY Consider the developmental, cultural, and linguistic appropriateness of the learning environment and your teaching practices for each child. Offer meaningful, relevant, and appropriately challenging activities across all interests and abilities.

Extending Children's Learning

What can you do to make sure your interactions, environment, and learning activities provide the types of teachable moments that Sonya had with Todd? Here are some ideas to extend children's learning in the moment:

> Structure a high-quality learning environment based on babies' and toddlers' development and interests. Provide a variety of materials to

encourage children to explore (e.g., toys that go in and out, busy boxes, blocks, nesting cups), and make sure nonmobile infants can reach and explore them. Change materials regularly to offer novel experiences.

> Include meaningful and representative materials that reflect children's cultures and languages (books, play props, blankets, baskets, and so on). This ensures that children see themselves reflected in the learning environment, enabling them to integrate new knowledge with familiar and culturally relevant materials.

> Slow down, wait, and watch what children are doing. Think about how, when, and why you want to interact with the child to make the most of opportunities to extend learning.

> Watch for both verbal and nonverbal responses to promote back-and-forth conversational interaction.

> Ask questions or wonder, even with babies—"Oh, what's happening? You are touching the busy box. I wonder what will happen when you push that button."

> Provide verbal support and modeling to extend children's exploration of materials and experiences.

> Offer specific information or guidance when children need help understanding concepts. For example, to encourage a child's understanding of cause and effect, you might say, "When you move your hand this way, the toy makes a rattling sound."

> Help children name and understand concepts by verbally labeling things like color, shape, sound, size, letters, numbers, and feelings. Be available to participate as children begin to enjoy imaginary play. Ask children, "What should I be? What should I do?" Follow their lead, adding context or vocabulary in the setting of their play. Respond to children's prompts or ideas, offering props to enrich the pretend scenario, such as suggesting the addition of blocks to serve as groceries in dramatic play about shopping.

> Promote a language-rich environment by narrating children's play and describing children's exploration and discoveries. Connect descriptive words with nouns: "Prisha, you're holding a small soft ball that rolls slowly. Flynn has the large rubber ball that bounces very high."

> Use children's home languages and English in the learning environment whenever possible. If you are not fluent in a child's home language, learn frequently used words and phrases to support your language interactions.

You may think of other ways to extend and build on your interactions with infants and toddlers. The key to teachable moments is that teachers modify activities in the moment to add expanded opportunities for learning, practicing, and refining new skills. Intentional teachers use these strategies in existing routines and activities. They may make it look simple, but these expansions and extensions to activities have big implications for the way infants and toddlers understand and make sense of the world around them.

Strategies to Try

You may remember a teacher who gave you a chance to practice new skills and provided hands-on support while you were learning. How can you provide similar support to infants and toddlers as they learn new skills?

> Be present and engage with children throughout the day to capitalize on teachable moments. Stop, watch, and take note of what children are interested in, what they are able to do, and what they seem interested in learning how to do.

> Promote critical thinking. Talk about what children are doing using descriptive language, novel vocabulary, and full sentences to offer the information needed to facilitate new understandings.

> Use simple explanations and reasoning to help children understand why things happen or to evaluate a choice: "Zuri, if you are coming down the slide you need to sit on your bottom. If you try to climb down with your feet, I think you might lose your balance and fall."

These language supports can turn any moment into a teachable moment. Infant and toddler teachers provide explicit language experiences that extend and expand children's learning. They do this in developmentally appropriate ways, with the developmental timing that supports individual children, and in daily teachable moments.

ALLYSON DEAN, EdD, is a former senior content specialist for Zero to Three and has worked in various roles to provide technical assistance to states on infant and toddler professional development and policy issues.

LINDA GROVES GILLESPIE, MS, has worked in the field of early education for the past 40 years, providing professional development about the importance of the first three years of life.

CHAPTER 17

"You're Okay" May Not Be Okay

Using Emotion Language to Promote Toddlers' Social and Emotional Development

Elizabeth K. King

Rowan is toddling back and forth on the carpet during free play. He follows his teacher as she moves around the room. As tears roll down his cheeks, coupled with soft sobs and unintelligible vocalizations, he reaches up with his arms above his head as if to say, "Pick me up, please?" Rowan's bids for attention from his teacher are met with, "You're okay." Each time a sob escapes from his small toddler frame, his teacher says one of the following: "You're okay." "You're fine."

Physically speaking, Rowan *is* okay, but it is clear he does not feel okay. His sobs, vocalizations, and bids for physical proximity do not decrease with each assurance that he is "okay." Rather, Rowan's emotional expression increases slightly with each conversational turn. Rowan resigns himself to a cycle of following his teacher, requesting to be soothed, giving up, then trying again.

Many toddlers, like Rowan, are not able to redirect themselves from the big feelings they experience throughout the day to engage and reengage with their learning environment. Often when children are emotionally aroused but unable to regulate their emotions, they internalize their feelings and reduce their emotional expression (Rowan giving up), or they escalate in their expression (Rowan's reaching, tears, and vocalizations). In the case of internalizing emotions, when children reduce their expression of emotion, they remain just as physiologically aroused (Fabes et al. 2001) but do not have an alternate way of managing their feelings. In escalation or internalization, young children's subsequent behaviors can limit their engagement with their community of learners (Mejia & Hoglund 2016; Mohamed 2018). An escalation in emotional expression may not be harmful up to a point, because emotions are learning opportunities. However, a more developmentally appropriate goal is for children to learn strategies to manage and express their emotions through warm, attentive teacher responses.

Using emotion-minimizing language with children in distress, such as "You're okay" or "You're fine, shush," sends the message that emotions (usually what adults consider negative emotions) are neither respected nor functional. This type of language can increase the likelihood that a toddler starts to internalize their emotions or exhibit behaviors unhelpful to their own and others' learning environments. It may also dampen their ability to feel secure to express emotions and practice ways to express emotions appropriately. For example, it takes many missteps to realize that lashing out at a peer to obtain a toy is not the most beneficial strategy to meet their goals. The social world of the early childhood classroom is ripe with opportunities for educators to support toddlers' social and emotional competence—opportunities missed in Rowan's case when the teacher tried to convince Rowan that he was "okay."

In this chapter, I describe social and emotional competence in toddlerhood and the importance of facilitating it in classrooms. Then, I offer strategies and activities to help early childhood teachers support toddlers' social and emotional development through their use of *emotion language*, which is verbal speech that refers to one's own or another's emotional state. In addition, I discuss an anti-oppressive approach to emotion language in classrooms.

Toddlers' Social and Emotional Competence

Throughout toddlerhood—from the second year of life through the third year of life—children transition from relying solely on caregivers for emotion regulation to developing their own skills to self-regulate. During this transition, toddlers are fairly reliant on caregivers to assist in emotion regulation as they learn to navigate their social worlds (Denham 2019; Sameroff 2010). Negotiating social interactions requires social and emotional competence, which includes the ability to identify emotions of self and other (often at the same time), understand causes and effects of emotion, and exhibit appropriate ways to express emotion to attain social goals (Denham, Bassett, & Wyatt 2007; Eisenberg, Cumberland, & Spinrad 1998). Social and emotional competence in early childhood increases toddlers' well-being (Giske et al. 2018), later peer acceptance and friendships (Ladd & Sechler 2013), and school adjustment (Bardack & Widen 2019).

Language Strategies for Supporting Social and Emotional Development

Humans create meaning around how their body responds to feelings or emotions, in part, through language (Lindquist, MacCormack, & Shablack 2015). Toddlers are in the process of learning the words associated with internal feelings, and learning vocabulary to associate with specific feelings is a helpful tool in toddlers' social and emotional toolbox (Brownell et al. 2013; Ornaghi et al. 2017). Classrooms can be language-rich spaces in which early childhood educators intentionally use language to help toddlers grow in their understanding and expression of emotions in social contexts. The language that teachers use in reaction to, and in more general discussion of, emotions can influence developing toddlers' understanding of emotions in social contexts. For example, you can respond to a toddler fighting with a peer over a toy by using language that simply stops or redirects the behavior ("We keep our hands to ourselves" or "Gentle touches"). You also can promote emotion understanding by stating aloud the emotion behind a behavior and providing an appropriate

alternative ("You're *frustrated* that you can't play with the train right now. Let's play with the trucks until Alanna is done with the train"). Research involving parents and early childhood educators demonstrates that emotion language relates to children's emotion knowledge (ability to accurately identify emotions) and prosocial behavior (helping and comforting) (Denham, Ferrier, & Bassett 2020; Ornaghi et al. 2017).

 Providing sensitive support and encouragement when children are frustrated or upset strengthens skills for self-regulation and emotion competence. In these moments, teachers help children solve problems with support and learn to use language to express their feelings.

Teachers' verbal responses to toddlers' emotions, such as "You look upset," are considered *contingent reactions* to the emotions (Denham, Bassett, & Wyatt 2007; Denham, Bassett, & Zinsser 2012). Contingent reactions influence how a toddler comes to understand their emotions, and they send messages to children about the validity of their emotions. Early childhood educators can use contingent reactions with emotion-affirming language ("You look sad—it's okay to feel sad") and guidance for appropriate management of emotions ("It's okay to cry" or "I feel angry sometimes too; it helps when I take deep breaths"). Such reactions help children understand their emotions and learn how to show appropriate external expressions (Yelinek & Grady 2019). Toddlers need sufficient space and support to practice strategies to regulate and express their emotions, as research has found that minimizing emotions may lead to less social and emotional competence in toddlers (King 2020).

Recommendations for Using Emotion-Affirming Language in Practice

Through play and other engaging activities, you can scaffold toddlers' social and emotional competence. For example, talk about emotions that are felt by book characters, toys, and peers ("The lion looks trapped under a branch! How do you think he feels?"). Play, outdoor time, and routines offer other opportunities to use emotion language to encourage toddlers to label and regulate their emotions. For example, you can facilitate toddlers' perspective taking during children's play by asking questions about emotions during a peer interaction, such as "How did that make you feel?" or "Do you see your friend is sad now that you knocked over his blocks?" If a child cautiously approaches the slide outdoors, you might say, "It's okay to feel scared of something new." Even during daily routines such as hand washing or brushing teeth, you can demonstrate that emotions are often caused by a particular situation: "I'm feeling a bit upset today after my dog chewed up my shoes this morning."

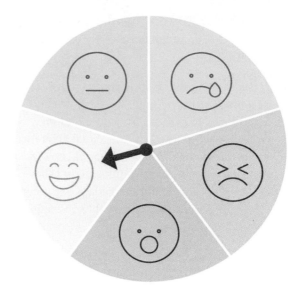

Here are recommended strategies for using positive emotion language that will support toddlers' social and emotional competence:

> Label, ask questions, and explain. Examine potential causes of toddlers' emotions during interactions. For example, when a toddler enters the classroom beaming, you might ask, "What's making you so happy today?"

> Discuss. Use book characters, puppets, and peer situations to facilitate toddlers' vocabulary about feelings and perspective taking. While reading a book, describe and imitate the main character's facial expression and connect this to emotion terms by saying, "Look at the turtle's eyebrows. They are furrowed like this. My eyebrows look like that when I feel mad." This can be done using any book; the book does not have to be focused on emotions.

> Select a book that teaches emotions. Here are a few to start with: *The Feelings Book*, by Todd Parr; *Baby Faces*, by Margaret Miller; *When I Am/ Cuando Estoy*, by Gladys Rosa-Mendoza; and *The Way I Feel*, by Janan Cain.

> Respect all emotions. Validate feelings ("It's okay to feel mad") without diminishing them ("Stop being mad"). Acknowledge in verbal and nonverbal ways children's feelings across the spectrum of emotions.

> Act out emotions using props and other visual supports. Create a feelings wheel such as shown on this page by cutting a circle from paper or cardstock. Label evenly divided sections with emotion words like *happy, sad,* or *disgusted*. Illustrate with facial expressions to represent the feelings. Attach a spinning pointer in the center (a paper clip will work). Ask the children to spin the

pointer. When it lands on an emotion, describe the emotion and ask the children to show that emotion with their whole bodies (as toddlers often do).

> Reflect on and describe your own emotions. Comments such as "I love the chilly fall weather because it makes me feel calm and safe" help children understand that people have emotions for a variety of reasons.

Considering the Intersection of Identity and Emotion: Gender and Race

Social and cultural contexts influence how children and adults come to understand emotions. Strong connections exist between social identities and emotions. Adults convey beliefs based on cultural expectations to children through their language about emotions.

For example, early childhood educators' responses and reactions to girls may differ from their responses and reactions to boys, based on cultural views. Boys' expressions of anger may be interpreted as appropriate ("Boys will be boys") based on societal expectations, whereas boys' expressions of sadness may be interpreted as inappropriate ("Boys don't cry"). Such gendered narratives directly and indirectly send messages to young children about the types of emotions that are acceptable for boys (as opposed to girls) to express. This may translate into teachers allowing boys' anger and dismissing their sadness (King 2020).

Indeed, studies of emotion socialization practices in classrooms have been found to differ by a child's gender (Denham, Bassett, & Zinsser 2012; King 2020) and align with overarching societal differences in power or status due to gender (Chaplin, Cole, & Zahn-Waxler 2005). Although adults might believe that they are preparing children to adapt to their social worlds through gendered practices, they instead may create emotional distress.

Our responses to emotions stem from our perceptions of emotions, which are affected by the narratives we have internalized about social groups. Along with gender, race is another social identity that intersects with children's developing social and emotional competence. Research suggests that emotions are discussed in Black communities differently than in White communities and as a means to prepare Black children for systemic and individual bias they may experience (Dunbar et al. 2017). For example, the documented overrepresentation of Black children in the rates of school suspension, even in early childhood settings, may be in part because Black children's emotions are viewed as angrier and more like the emotions of an adult than White children's emotions (Goff et al. 2014; Halberstadt et al. 2020).

Early childhood educators are called to "create early learning environments that equitably distribute learning opportunities by helping all children experience responsive interactions that nurture their full range of social, emotional, cognitive, physical, and linguistic abilities . . ." (NAEYC 2019, 5). To examine potential biases, teachers can ask themselves the following questions:

> What are emotion expressions that I expect of a toddler? Why do I expect them?

> In my classroom, who do I feel most often expresses emotions, such as anger, frustration, or sadness?

> Who do I feel most comfortable with when they express sadness (or happiness, anger, or frustration)?

> Who do I expect or want to feel happiness (or sadness or anger) most often?

> When an individual child expresses frustration or anger, what is my initial reaction? Does this differ across children?

> What are emotion expressions that concern me or that I think are inappropriate for a toddler to display? Why do they concern me? What do I do next?

It is important for educators to reflect on the *why* of their responses to toddlers' emotion to ensure that they are not operating under false assumptions regarding children's gender, race, or other aspects of their social identities. By paying attention to the emotion language they use and constantly checking their perceptions of children, teachers can ensure they provide supportive responses to the emotions of each and every child.

ELIZABETH K. KING, PhD, is an associate professor of child and family development at Missouri State University in Springfield. Her research focuses on emotion language and its relation to young children's social and emotional development, situated within sociohistorical context.

CHAPTER 18

We Put Paper on the Floor
Supporting the Emergent Literacy Skills of Infants and Toddlers

Dilshad Tolliver

Infants and toddlers change so quickly in a short time. They have a sense of wonder and excitement, and as they develop and learn, their interests continue to grow and emerge. At our school, we provide many experiences to support toddlers' early literacy development. Throughout the classroom, children have access to many open-ended writing and painting materials as well as books.

Teachers closely observe the children as they navigate materials and engage in a wide range of experiences that support early literacy development. We then record these observations so we can expand on the children's continued interests throughout the other areas of the classroom and developmental domains. Teachers meet weekly to discuss what the children are interested in, determine what activities we should add to our curriculum guide, and set goals for each individual child according to their developmental age.

We then email families the general plan for the week, ask for their input, and encourage them to share pictures of their children engaged in play and exploration at home (like cooking together) so we can strengthen connections between home and school. These photos are used to extend children's at-home explorations in the classroom and as part of our documentation. By inviting families to participate in this way, we build stronger home-school relationships and foster more robust family engagement.

Writing and Drawing in an Infant and Toddler Classroom

One year, the infants and toddlers in our mixed-age classroom of 12- to 24-month-olds showed a strong interest in early literacy activities, particularly in exploring many different drawing, painting, and writing tools. What follows are a few different scenes that unfolded.

A 10-month-old boy is able to grasp writing and drawing materials. We support his natural curiosity of writing and print by allowing him to sit with some of the older children who are manipulating similar materials and writing ideas. The infant learns more about the tools as he experiments with manipulating them.

A few infants in the library center sit and flip through the pages in board books, looking at the pictures and print. Meanwhile, some of the older toddlers are going through books more deliberately, naming objects and characters they notice as they go.

A few children who are 12 to 18 months old experiment with removing the lids from containers of paint and placing them back on. They are entering the sensorimotor stage of writing and drawing, which moves beyond exploration of the materials to the beginnings of mark making, including dots, zigzags, and whorls. The children use their entire fist to grasp utensils and incorporate their whole arm in the mark-making process. We teachers notice that the children are starting to show a preference for which hand to write with, and we continue to support them as they make this preference known.

A few children between the ages of 18 months and 3 years graduate from the sensorimotor stage of writing to the preoperational stage. This means that their writing transforms from nonfigural graphics (such as scribbling and wavy lines on the page simply for the joy of writing) to purposeful and consistent strings of circles or pseudo letters.

One older toddler starts to use her drawings to represent objects and ideas. She makes connections to items used for provocation (letters, pictures, and other items set out by the teacher) and often engages in private speech (talking out loud to herself) while exploring writing. She sings the alphabet when letters are present; discusses her friends, teachers, and family when pictures are displayed; and even goes one step further by recalling people, places, and things to give a deeper meaning to her strokes.

Throughout the weeks, we collect the children's writing work samples and put them on display in our classroom at the children's eye-level. Tommy, an older toddler, points to his work and says, "Mine." The teacher responds, "Yes, Tommy, this is your work. What did you write about?" Tommy looks at his scribbles and says, "Work." Another child who cannot verbally express her thoughts yet in words points to the display and smiles.

At the beginning of the year, simple writing and drawing tools are placed on tables in the writing center for the children to sit and use. The utensils include wide crayons and markers that young toddlers can easily grasp as they develop their small muscle control. Soon, however, we notice the older toddlers grow bored and begin to write on the furniture, floor, and walls of the classroom.

Observing this repeated behavior compels our teaching team to consider how we can continue to foster the children's love of writing while also focusing their energies on more planful learning experiences. After some brainstorming, we adjust our thinking and come up with a few ideas for accommodating the children's interest in exploring writing in ways that are less restrictive. For a different perspective and an environmental change, we tape paper on the classroom floor, set up easels, and provide chalk outdoors. At the easels, there are paintbrushes in a range of colors and sizes for children to use as they explore mixing colors and making brushstrokes on paper. Gradually, we introduce oil pastels, colored pencils, and ink pens for the children to explore different textures and the way these tools leave marks on paper.

Children's Early Exploration of Writing and Reading

We view children as readers and writers, and we strive to provide materials to support this. The children in our classroom explore writing materials in different ways based on their age and developmental level;

however, they are all developing important skills. At first, children's writing involves very simple explorations. Infants and toddlers consider writing and drawing the same. They cannot differentiate between the two until they are older and can recognize something as a picture to be drawn or as letters to be written. Regardless, their scribbles are meaningful to them as writers.

Using materials such as paints and wide crayons, children can strengthen the small muscles later needed for writing, explore ways to make marks on paper, and express themselves through making these marks. As children begin to grow and develop, these simple marks become more controlled and complex, and they incorporate various features of conventional written language. Their writing samples often include circles, dots, vertical lines, horizontal lines, and repeated marks on the page. When children describe what their writings say, they illustrate their understanding that marks and letters represent something. Observations like these demonstrate that literacy skills develop early; therefore, it is important that children of all ages be given many opportunities to explore drawing and writing.

When children have a lot of experiences with print in books and in their environment, they use what they observe about letters and words in their scribbling and writing. Literacy experiences like flipping book pages, looking at print, and retelling stories to themselves and others are important in helping young children develop critical skills, including understanding the purpose of books and recognizing print to have meaning, even at a young age. In our classroom, we constantly see connections between children looking at print as they flip through books and the marks they make with crayons and other materials to represent print.

Early literacy skills begin to develop long before young children begin formal writing and reading instruction in elementary school. Early literacy development does not simply happen; rather, it is part of a social process, embedded in children's relationships with others. This is one of the many reasons that the home-school connection is especially important when teaching in an infant and toddler classroom. It is people who make reading and writing interesting and meaningful to young children. Family members, caregivers, and teachers serve as models who demonstrate the use of materials, provide materials, and offer encouragement to children in their use of literacy materials.

EQUITY Offering meaningful, relevant, and appropriately challenging activities across all interests and abilities communicates value to children. Teachers consider the developmental, cultural, and linguistic appropriateness of the learning environment and teaching practices for each child.

Connections to Developmentally Appropriate Practice

As part of our school philosophy, we believe that all children are capable, competent learners and that every age group should be given the opportunity to explore the materials in their environment, especially the youngest of learners. As we think about toddler early literacy and writing, we see many connections to the guidelines and principles in NAEYC's position statement on developmentally appropriate practice (NAEYC 2020a). Here are just a few:

> We meet weekly to discuss our curriculum plan and how we might adjust for children's interests. We also respond to children's interest in exploring writing materials in different ways and incorporate this into our weekly planning (guideline 5).

> We share our plans with families and offer them ways to, in turn, share what they are experiencing at home with their children to strengthen learning across home and school settings in ways that are mutually supportive (guideline 2).

> We understand that toddlers experience literacy in a connected way and see connections between book reading and writing explorations (principle 7).

> We understand that young children learn through exploration and play and that drawing on the floor is a way of exploring use of materials. We adjust how we offer writing materials based on children's explorations and interests (principle 5).

> We observe what children are doing and what we are offering, and we adjust how we organize materials. We also discuss the results and what individual children are doing to show us what they know about writing (guidelines 3 and 4).

As you think about your own work with infants and toddlers, perhaps there is a strategy, activity, or material from the vignettes shared in this chapter that you would like to try with the children. Consider how you might let children take the lead in exploring materials and adapt the activities to suit their needs and interests—and support their literacy learning in joyful ways!

DILSHAD TOLLIVER is an early childhood education specialist at the A. Sophie Rogers School for Early Learning at the Ohio State University in Columbus.

PART 5

Planning and Implementing an Engaging Curriculum to Achieve Meaningful Goals

RECOMMENDATIONS FROM THE DAP STATEMENT

The curriculum consists of the plans for the learning experiences through which children acquire knowledge, skills, abilities, and understanding. In developmentally appropriate practice, the curriculum helps young children achieve goals that are meaningful because they are culturally and linguistically responsive and developmentally and educationally significant. The curriculum does this through learning experiences that reflect what is known about young children in general and about each child in particular.

Xavier's father, Mr. Carter, connects the last two containers to the line of cardboard boxes. "We did it. We have an express train!" he exclaims. The teacher, Ms. Grace, adds a soft pillow to each box compartment and says, "All aboard! Climb on in. Let's get ready for the train ride." Willow and Daniel scramble in. "Where will we go? Who will we visit?" asks Ms. Grace. "Gamma," says Xavier. "What do you take to Grandma's house?" asks Ms. Grace. "Socks!" yells Willow. "Backpack," says Daniel. "Yes, your mama packs clothes in your backpack," says Ms. Grace. Jeremiah and Xavier climb into the train cars. Mr. Carter shouts, "Hold on tight. Choo, choo, choo."

In this urban program, the toddlers ride the bus with their families and take a train to visit family members. Ms. Grace reads picture books that show children riding the subway, bus, and train. For today's pretend train trip, Ms. Grace provides water bottles, small notebooks, and snacks for the children to pack. This kind of integrated curriculum invites family participation, engages the children's questions and lived experiences, and gets them excited about learning.

Curriculum for infants and toddlers refers to the routines and experiences that support children's development and learning. The setting, play activities, songs, materials, and daily events, along with the supportive relationships among adults and children, are part of a curriculum that promotes learning across all areas of development. Educators work with families to create social, emotional, and language experiences that are culturally and linguistically responsive—and that are meaningful to children.

Developmentally appropriate curriculum for infants and toddlers is active, relational, and play based. It focuses on early literacy and rich social interactions. Infants enjoy dramatic stories and puppet play, and they depend on teachers to label emotions and help them solve problems. Books for infants and toddlers reflect experiences they know and enjoy and introduce them to new people, places, and ideas. These rich experiences in vocabulary and concept learning also support future learning across all subject areas.

Curriculum is used as a flexible framework. While teachers plan daily play activities for infants and toddlers, they also adapt what they plan by responding to children during moment-by-moment interactions. In addition to setting specific learning goals, they follow children's lead to connect with their individual play interests, engagement levels, and social and physical needs.

Creativity and self-expression are encouraged through interactive games, rhythms and rhymes, songs and lullabies, whole body play, and creative art activities. These pursuits help children develop language, social, and physical skills as well as confidence, pride, and identification with their families and cultures. Creative experiences are designed to fit with children's interests and attention spans and offer a range of challenges so all children can participate successfully.

During indoor and outdoor play, educators introduce opportunities for children to develop their thinking skills and solve problems. They invite children to observe and learn about science and nature through daily activities such as watering plants. They use rich, descriptive words to encourage vocabulary and concept development. STEM (science, technology, engineering, and mathematics) skills are integrated through many kinds of active play, as children express curiosity and experiment to understand how things work.

In Part 5, you will find stories and examples that include practical steps to prepare curriculum that address learning goals across all developmental domains.

READ AND REFLECT

As you read the chapters in this section, consider and evaluate your own classroom practices using these reflection questions.

"Curriculum Considerations for Multilingual Infants and Toddlers" describes strategies to promote positive relationships, provide oral language support, strengthen home languages, and collaborate with multilingual families. **Consider:** How can you support different trajectories of expressive language, and what strategies can encourage and support the children you teach? What changes can you make in your practice to work with multilingual infants and toddlers and their families? How can you include expressive modeling, gestures, and active movement to engage children?

"When in Doubt, Reach Out: Teaming Strategies for Inclusive Settings" follows the experiences of a new teacher in an inclusive toddler classroom. It provides an overview of early intervention processes, essential team members, and effective strategies for collaboration. **Consider:** Think about all the adults who support the growth and learning of the children in your program. How and when do you communicate and provide feedback? How can you partner with others more effectively? How can you apply what you learn about one child to the effectiveness of your teaching with other children?

"Exploring Outdoors: First Learning Experiences in Nature" links the joy of children's sensory immersion in nature experiences with the role of the teacher as guide to learning through meaningful conversation. The authors point out the ways sensory engagement outdoors leads to higher-level cognitive skills as children interact with the processes of the living world. **Consider:** What can you do to enhance children's access to nature and the outdoor spaces of your program? What else can you bring to the indoor and outdoor spaces to increase children's experiences with nature?

"Using the Environment and Materials as Curriculum for Promoting Exploration of Cause and Effect" illustrates how one teacher observes and builds on children's unique interests and curiosity about how things work to create meaningful emergent curriculum. **Consider:** How are you using tubes, ramps, and other open-ended materials to develop children's understanding of cause and effect? How can you invite children to experiment with and explore materials in new ways?

"Infant and Toddler STEAM: Supporting Interdisciplinary Experiences with Our Youngest Learners" shows how teachers promote cognitive and social skills that translate to meaningful engagement and learning, like reasoning, problem solving, and communication, and strengthen learning across areas of development. **Consider:** In what ways can you introduce STEAM (science, technology, engineering, art, and mathematics) activities that will build on children's natural curiosity, creativity, and interests?

NEXT STEPS

After reading Part 5, you'll be inspired to try some new approaches to curriculum planning or add to what you are already doing.

1. As you consider new ways to incorporate open-ended materials, which colleagues should be part of your planning conversation? What next steps would you like to take to include specific developmental and learning goals in your planning?

2. When you design curriculum, what parts do you think are nonnegotiable, and in what parts should you be flexible? What insights can you gain by observing children's responses to curriculum that can help you adjust future planning?

3. Consider new strategies to integrate curriculum planning and link skills across developmental domains. For instance, instead of focusing only on fine motor skills, what might result if you embed those skills as part of a project about visiting family members and friends? How can an integrated curriculum provide a more comprehensive, appropriately challenging, and engaging learning experience for the children?

References for the chapters in this part can be accessed online at NAEYC.org/books/focus-infants toddlers.

CHAPTER 19

Curriculum Considerations for Multilingual Infants and Toddlers

Irasema Salinas-González, Iliana Alanís, and María G. Arreguín

Ms. Norma, an English-dominant teacher, is the primary caregiver for three mobile infants in her Early Head Start center. She knows the three children and their families well because she cared for them in the young infant room last year. Her multilingual classroom reflects the contexts of many infant and toddler classrooms in her state. There is 9-month-old Yareli, raised by her Spanish-speaking grandmother; 10-month-old Thao, who lives with her two Vietnamese parents; and 11-month-old Nathan, who lives with his bilingual (English/Spanish) mom and grandparents.

Yareli arrives, carried by her grandmother. Ms. Norma greets them with a smile and a hand wave, saying, "Buenos días, Yareli!" in a rhythmical voice. "So glad you're here, amorcito [my love]!" Yareli smiles and stretches her arms toward Ms. Norma. As she does this, she drops a ball she is holding. Her grandmother says, "Yo me quedo con la pelota, la niña no la quiso soltar esta mañana" [I'll keep the ball. She did not want to let it go this morning]. The teacher gestures and says, "It's okay to bring the pelota [ball]." Yareli's grandmother smiles as the teacher takes her granddaughter. Ms. Norma holds Yareli's hand and waves with it: "Bye, bye, abuelita." She then asks Yareli, "Where's the ball, pelota?" as she pretends to look for it. Yareli soon looks at the ball, which is rolling on the floor. Ms. Norma also looks at the rolling ball and points to it while saying, "Look, your ball is rolling. It's rolling out the door!"

As they both smile and start heading toward the ball, a group of simultaneous bilingual toddlers (who are acquiring two or more languages from birth to age 3) walk by with their teacher, Mrs. Patty. There's 16-month-old Gil, 18-month-old Diego, 24-month-old Bianca, and 30-month-old Wen. They see the ball rolling and start to bounce and giggle. "Peota bica!" yells Gil. "Qua' bóng nay!" cheers Wen. Mrs. Patty acknowledges their observations of the ball by saying, "Si, la pelota roja rueda. A dónde se fue la pelota roja?" [Yes, the red ball rolls. Where did the red ball go?].

As Ms. Norma later plans to prepare the play environment, she considers how to add a collection of multisensory balls and thinks about helpful interactions that may expand her mobile infants' language. She also remembers the word *pelota* that Yareli's grandmother used and wonders what the ball is called in Vietnamese. Mrs. Patty remembers how excited her toddlers got when they encountered the rolling ball. She also thinks about the different words her toddlers used as the ball rolled by them.

This vignette demonstrates how intentional teachers consider children's social, cultural, and linguistic backgrounds when developing an engaging curriculum for multilingual infants and toddlers. Ms. Norma values the importance of building responsive relationships with children and families and uses these daily encounters to nurture children's social, emotional, and language development. Mrs. Patty understands that she needs to add to children's linguistic repertoire as she extends children's vocabulary ("Si, la pelota roja rueda. A donde se fue la pelota roja?") [Yes, the red ball rolls. Where did the red ball go?].

Authors' Note

In this chapter, we use the term *multilingual* interchangeably with *simultaneous bilingual* to refer to children who are exposed to and acquire more than one language in an early childhood setting during early development.

The first five years of a child's life are significant for language development (NASEM 2017). During these early years, families and communities are the primary sources for young children to learn about their world. They are also how children acquire language and learn about themselves and others (Alanís & Iruka 2023; Rogoff 2003).

According to the US Census Bureau (2021), nearly 22 percent of Americans speak languages other than English in their households, with 13 percent speaking Spanish at home. It is estimated that three-quarters of bilingually raised children hear the school language and another language at home (De Houwer 2021). Their learning needs differ from those of their monolingual peers and older children who learn a second or third language in formal school settings. Therefore, educators of multilingual infants and toddlers must consider how their work is developmentally, culturally, and linguistically appropriate for the children in their settings (NAEYC 2020a).

What Do We Know About Multilingual Infants and Toddlers?

Children have the capacity to learn multiple languages and communication patterns from birth (Otto 2018). But while multilingual infants and toddlers listen to two or more languages during their formative years, monolingual children listen to just one. Multilingual children therefore learn to engage in unique linguistic practices as part of their development and learning (Byers-Heinlein, Morin-Lessard, & Lew-Williams 2017). They make sense of the complexities of two languages just by listening to the sounds and rhythms of the languages and develop a unique linguistic repertoire comprising language skills in two or more languages (Bosch & Sebastián-Gallés 2001; D'Souza et al. 2020).

As a result, multilingual infants can differentiate between words in different languages as young as 20 months of age (Byers-Heinlein, Morin-Lessard, & Lew-Williams 2017). This indicates that children who grow up in multilingual contexts are not confused by the multiple linguistic systems they are exposed to. Instead, multilingual learners naturally activate the vocabulary of the language used in any particular setting.

Second or third language acquisition displays some similar patterns as native language acquisition. For example, bilingual infants experience comparable language milestones (cooing, babbling, first word) at about the same time as monolingual infants (De Houwer 2021; Hoff et al. 2012). Like all children,

multilingual infants and toddlers develop receptive language skills (listening) before they develop expressive language skills (speaking). Receptive language skills appear to emerge early, with infants as young as 10–13 months old recognizing familiar words in each of their languages (Poulin-Dubois, Brooker, & Polonia 2011). By age 3, children's receptive vocabulary is up to four times greater than their expressive vocabulary (Jalongo & Sobolak 2011).

In addition, learning to understand two or more languages often results in children using two languages within the same utterance (e.g., "¿Te gusta el doggy?" [Do you like the doggy?]). The multiple languages of a bilingual child will cross and influence one another during the acquisition and use of their languages. It is very common for multilingual learners to use all their language skills when speaking (e.g., "More leche" [More milk]). This complex pattern of code-switching is not evidence of confusion or language delay but a natural process in language development.

How Can Teachers Support Multilingual Language Development in Infants and Toddlers?

Teachers like Ms. Norma and Mrs. Patty know that infants and toddlers develop best within caring, responsive relationships regardless of their language background. However, they wonder how to plan an engaging curriculum that supports multilingual infants and toddlers. Let's explore some curricular components that support young children's multilingual development.

Promoting Responsive Relationships

Young multilingual infants and toddlers benefit from consistent responsive relationships with teachers and parents. Their social and emotional development is enhanced when they feel welcomed in the classroom. Yareli, the mobile infant in the opening vignette, and her teacher formed a secure relationship, as they have known each other since she was two months old. The infant extended her arms to be carried by her teacher, demonstrating feelings of trust. When there is continuity of care like this, teachers understand young children's languages and learning preferences and carefully use them to plan experiences that stimulate their interests (Shonkoff & Phillips 2000). Although both teachers in the opening vignette do not speak all their children's home languages, practicing continuity of care allows them to recognize the children's unique gestures, early vocalizations, and utterances. Infants and toddlers who are understood by their teachers feel safe and nurtured in a new linguistic environment. These positive relationships encourage young children to use their senses as they explore and learn.

Responsive teachers of multilingual young children engage in the following best practices:

> Communicate with families to learn about and respect cultural differences in caring for their young children.

> Learn children's individual cues for feeding, holding, changing, playing, and so on.

> Create routines and rituals when saying goodbye to family members, such as giving a kiss and waving goodbye.

> Talk, pause, and wait for infants and toddlers to respond verbally or nonverbally during daily routines such as feeding, diapering, and playing.

Although these practices are effective for all children, they are particularly significant for young multilingual learners who are experiencing their first formal setting away from home in a new linguistic and cultural environment.

Providing Oral Language Support

Responsive teachers of multilingual infants and toddlers focus on daily interactions and routines for supporting language and cognitive development. For example, both teachers in the opening vignette responded to the children's needs by following the children's interest in balls and using language to narrate the incident. Ms. Norma used the word *look* to secure joint attention, which is linked to language acquisition and important for relationship building. And both Ms. Norma and Mrs. Patty used language that was connected to the children's immediate focus

of attention—the rolling ball. This shared reference, the ball, became the center of their interaction. Teachers' gestures and facial expressions, along with the words they use to describe what children are focused on, help children learn new concepts and vocabulary (Otto 2019).

Young multilingual children require language partners for both language and cognitive development. Social interaction is a crucial factor in learning, and both children and adults can be conversational partners. Interactions that are warm and playful provide the basis for language development during infancy as young children learn conversational turn taking with responsive adults (Gonzalez-Mena 2010).

Supporting the Child's Home Language

Teachers of young multilingual children plan experiences that nurture and support their home language and culture. Ask families to teach you key words and commonly used phrases in the children's home language, such as words that demonstrate basic needs (*more, sleepy, hungry, afraid, sick*). You may also want to learn how to say the words that identify members of the child's family, such as *mother, father,* and *grandmother*. Learning words of endearment and familiar objects also validates children's home languages. Greet families in their home language so they feel welcomed and comfortable interacting with you (Weitzman & Greenberg 2002). Ask family members to audiotape themselves reading a story in their home language and then play it for the child as you and the child look at the book together. You may also ask families to teach you finger plays and rhymes from their home language.

DAP Like Ms. Norma and Mrs. Patty, responsive educators support children's curiosity and engagement with the daily natural events and patterns they observe. They plan interaction, vocabulary, and questions to use with children during play.

Strategies and Tips for Working with Multilingual Infants and Toddlers

The following teaching practices support the development of language and communication skills in multilingual infants and toddlers:

> Talk about what the children are doing and talk about what you are doing. Mrs. Patty verbally maps what children are doing or seeing by saying, "You're rolling the ball on the ramp."

> Use gestures, facial expressions, or simple signs with words. Ms. Norma asks Thao if she's hungry by touching her lips.

> Read interactively one-on-one or in small informal groups. Encourage children to mouth, handle, and explore books.

> Engage in action songs, rhymes, and finger plays. Make up songs about daily happenings in the classroom, such as "Where is the sock, where is the sock? Here it is, here it is."

> Use "parentese." Infants prefer a high-pitched tone of voice that adults tend to use naturally with infants (Ramírez, Lytle, & Kuhl 2020). Consider cultural norms and observe families interacting with their infants to understand their communication patterns.

> Create predictable routines cued by oral language. For example, sing a special song to let children know that it will be time to clean up or that a transition is coming.

> Expand on what children say. For example, if the child says "Mama," you might say, "I know you miss Mama. She'll be coming soon."

Conclusion

Children's early years are formative for language development and set the stage for later academic and social outcomes. Although there are universal aspects of language development, educators must understand the differences between monolingual and multilingual children to reflect an equity lens in the early education setting. Responsive teachers ask children questions, respond to their vocalizations, and engage in positive talk that encourages children to learn and use their entire linguistic repertoire. The more words young children hear in any language, the larger their vocabularies (NASEM 2017). When teachers integrate multisensory activities that follow children's interests, language and cognition will develop. Ultimately, when teachers understand and draw on social and cultural influences that support powerful language learning, they are better positioned to engage in equitable and inclusive language practices (Alanís & Iruka, with Friedman 2021).

IRASEMA SALINAS-GONZÁLEZ, EdD, is an associate professor of early care and early childhood studies at the University of Texas Rio Grande Valley.

ILIANA ALANÍS, PhD, is a professor of early childhood and elementary education at the University of Texas–San Antonio.

MARÍA G. ARREGUÍN, EdD, is a professor of early childhood and elementary education at the University of Texas–San Antonio.

CHAPTER 20

When in Doubt, Reach Out
Teaming Strategies for Inclusive Settings

Christine M. Spence, Deserai Miller, Catherine Corr, Rosa Milagros Santos, and Brandie Bentley

Genevieve, a new teacher in the toddler room at an early childhood center, is excited to meet her coworkers and the children in her classroom. Over the next several weeks, Genevieve spends time getting to know the children and their families.

Alex is a 2-year-old in Genevieve's class. Alex currently receives early intervention services due to concerns about his communication and social and emotional development. Alex's family has shared his Individualized Family Service Plan (IFSP) with Joy, the center director, and Genevieve has reviewed it. Still, she has several questions, including how to help Alex play with his peers and communicate more effectively when he is upset. Dani, a speech-language pathologist, works with Alex every Thursday at the center, and Maura is an occupational therapist who sees Alex at home on Monday evenings. Genevieve knows that Alex's family has a social worker as part of the team, but she doesn't know when they meet.

Genevieve wants to support Alex's participation in the classroom. She wants to work with the specialists, but she isn't sure where to begin. She talks with Joy, and they decide to ask Alex's parents, Audrey and Xavier, if they can schedule a meeting.

Inclusive Settings for Young Children

Inclusive settings are those that include children with and without disabilities. Children with developmental delays or disabilities participate in many inclusive community activities, such as early learning programs, park district programs, and library story times. The defining features of inclusive programs for young children include access to community settings, full and active participation in the activities within those environments, and administrative support necessary

for participation (DEC/NAEYC 2009). Today's inclusive early childhood settings provide robust programs for all early learners, including those with disabilities or developmental delays. Strong, consistent collaboration among educators, early interventionists, and family members is necessary for high-quality inclusion (NPDCI 2009). Having access to professional development, consultation, and other resources helps educators view inclusion more positively, and it also creates positive experiences for the child (Muccio et al. 2014; Yu 2019).

For example, to ensure that Alex fully engages in Genevieve's classroom, ongoing and individualized assistance is essential. This will be provided by Alex's family, his early intervention team, and Genevieve. Additionally, as the center director, Joy can offer the time and resources for Genevieve to participate in professional development and to plan, consult, and reflect with other members of Alex's team.

An Overview of Early Intervention and Team Members

Early intervention is a federally supported program for families who have a child under 36 months of age with a developmental delay or disability (Individuals with Disabilities Education Act [IDEA] 2004). Early intervention may not always look the same across states, but there are some common characteristics:

> A service coordinator is responsible for ensuring that each eligible child receives all the services listed on their IFSP.

> The IFSP includes the child's developmental levels, family-identified outcomes, the services for which the child is eligible that will assist with meeting those outcomes, and the service providers who will support the family.

> Early interventionists form a team to support the family in meeting IFSP outcomes. (See "Who Is on the Early Intervention Team, and What Do They Do?" for information for families about potential team members.)

In some states, one team member is assigned as the primary person to work with a family, with guidance and contributions from other team members. In other states, multiple team members work with the child and family on a regular basis. Regardless of the service model, early interventionists work around a child's daily and weekly routines, both at home and in the community. They partner with the family and with community entities to support the family in meeting IFSP outcomes (Keilty 2016; Pletcher & Younggren 2013; Raver & Childress 2015). For example, an IFSP outcome could include being able to express wants and needs verbally or by using an alternative communication system, or it could include being able to participate in mealtime routines with the family. Each IFSP will list child- and family-specific strategies to help meet the outcomes; strategies will not be the same for different families even if the overarching outcome is similar.

Elements of Effective Communication and Collaboration

Early childhood educators in both center- and home-based settings can team with early interventionists. Indeed, participating as a team member on a child's IFSP is a vital step toward effective collaboration. For a child with a disability to succeed in an inclusive classroom, continual communication and regular meetings are critical.

Who Is on the Early Intervention Team, and What Do They Do?

Profession	Area(s) of Focus
Occupational therapist (Maura)	Motor development, self-help skills, sensory and regulatory procession
Physical therapist	Motor development, use of adaptive equipment (if needed)
Service coordinator (Sonia)	Identification of team and monitoring of implementation of services on IFSP
Social worker (Tyra)	Parent-child relationship, attachment, resources
Special instruction provider (also known by other terms, such as child development specialist, developmental therapist, early intervention teacher)	General development, cognitive development, play, social interaction; plans and collaboratively implements modifications and accommodations (if needed)
Speech-language pathologist (Dani)	Expressive language (talking, sign language, augmentative communication, picture communication systems), receptive language (understanding), articulation
Early childhood teacher (Genevieve)	Daily care and learning experiences, play, social interaction; plans curriculum and evaluates outcomes; collaboratively implements accommodations (if needed)

When all the members of a team—including the family—work together, individualized services are consistent across multiple settings. Children who receive supports in multiple settings have interconnected opportunities to practice and make progress on skills that enhance their engagement in everyday routines and learning experiences (Keilty 2016; Raver & Childress 2015). Each member of the team plays a role in collaboration and communication so that a child experiences appropriate adaptations and strategies for positive learning and growth to occur (Blackwell & Dunn 2016; Hart Barnett & O'shaugnessy 2015).

DAP Children with disabilities need educators who do not label them or isolate them from their peers and who are prepared to work with them and their families to develop their potential.

Strategies for Effective Communication and Collaboration

Because of the number of individuals on an IFSP team, efficient communication is essential. Five key strategies can foster effective communication, which can in turn lead to fruitful collaboration.

Defining Roles

Genevieve knows that Alex and his family are supported by several professionals, but she is not sure about each person's unique role and focus with Alex. Genevieve is particularly confused with outcomes related to Alex's social and emotional development. She would like clarification on the strategies that Maura suggests and how these are similar to or different from the information Tyra, the social worker, is sharing with Alex's family. Also, Genevieve is unsure of what interaction Sonia, the service coordinator, has with the rest of the team. As Genevieve reviews Alex's IFSP, she makes notes of questions that she will ask Audrey and Xavier when she has the opportunity to discuss the plan and people involved.

Everyone working on a team has a role, but those roles may not be readily evident. Some roles are clear, such as the speech-language pathologist who is responsible for providing strategies, activities, and materials to promote language and communication. Other roles, such as social work or occupational therapy, may be unclear, so establishing responsibilities in the initial stages of an IFSP prevents confusion and ensures that follow-through occurs in all areas.

Exchanging Information

When Genevieve first meets with Alex's family, she asks them to complete the necessary consent forms for her center. She also asks the family to sign consents with all of Alex's early interventionists so she can discuss Alex's goals and progress with everyone on the team. She shares with the family information about the daily class schedule and ideas that she has to help Alex feel part of the classroom. She mentions that there may occasionally be classroom visitors and asks for input from Alex's parents on how to make sure Alex is comfortable with new people. Genevieve also informs Audrey and Xavier that Joy is very supportive and has provided her with information and resources. Additionally, she plans to take a short class on inclusion and hopes to learn more about supporting children with developmental delays.

Once she obtains consent and has the appropriate contact information, she asks each team member questions, such as their preferred means of communication, the frequency with which they would like to communicate, and the best times of day to communicate via phone, email, or in person. During these conversations, Genevieve also inquires about service delivery and gathers more information related to Alex's development. She'll use this information to plan activities in the classroom.

Because Genevieve is relatively unfamiliar with the IFSP process, she asks questions related to it. Genevieve notices that a particular strategy listed on the IFSP—providing Alex a quiet space with no distractions—will not work in the classroom setting, so she invites Maura, the occupational therapist, to observe. Together, they brainstorm alternative strategies and ideas. These include having soothing and familiar objects available for Alex and rearranging the classroom so he has a space he can safely go to when he is overwhelmed. Both Genevieve and Maura feel like this visit in the classroom created an opportunity for more meaningful collaboration to occur, and Alex's parents are excited to learn about the conversation between the two. They support the strategies identified through this collaboration.

Effective communication depends upon having consent to share information among members of the IFSP team and other important adults in the child's daily life. Early interventionists and educators must receive consent from the child's legal guardian for this to happen. It is important to understand which consent forms are necessary within an organization and also to learn what consent forms are needed from other providers on the team. Many times, a release of information needs to be completed for all team members who plan to communicate. If parental consent to share information is difficult to obtain, team members should listen to the family's concerns and have an open conversation about why consent to exchanging this information will help the child. Often, concerns are alleviated by explaining who will have access to what types of information and how it will be used. Parents should know that they can revoke consent at any time.

Once consent forms have been signed, team members should identify the best way to communicate with each other and with families. With that information, each team member can regularly call, text, or email each other. They also can observe how the child learns and interacts with others in a variety of settings. Because each team member is working toward the same goals and outcomes—but providing different services to reach these goals—all team members can seek understanding about service delivery and the child's needs, strengths, interests, and other assets shown in different contexts or settings.

Using Communication Logs

Alex has a large team, and Genevieve finds herself communicating with many different people. She recalls that Alex's parents expressed a preference for communication to be on paper. It allows them to write information more easily, rather than having to remember to log into a website with a digital notebook. So Genevieve uses a paper notebook to begin a communication log. After each conversation with a team member, she documents the date, time, and person she spoke with, along with a brief summary of the discussion. The communication log is stored in Alex's backpack in his cubby.

Genevieve herself comes to rely on the communication log as a reference for her notes and ongoing planning. Other team members use it to catch up on what has happened during the day at the center. Tyra (the social worker) usually sees Alex and his family at home, but she occasionally visits the center to assist Alex there. When she does, she communicates face-to-face with Genevieve, as well as in the notebook. Alex's parents also contribute to the conversation by writing in the log so that the other team members know what is working well at home and in community settings. Joy helps in these efforts by providing Genevieve with time during the day to write in the notebook and read what others wrote.

A clear and agreed-upon communication strategy encourages all team members to contribute and stay informed. It also ensures that the sole responsibility for sharing information does not rest on just one person, particularly the parent. This communication system can be physical (a spiral notebook) or digital (a shared document on a password-protected account). The primary considerations are ease of use and privacy. (For a sample communication log used with multiple team members, visit NAEYC.org/books/focus-infants-toddlers.)

Scheduling Regular Meetings with All Team Members

While communication among the family, early learning program, and early intervention providers should occur on a regular basis, convening a formal IFSP meeting offers the time and space for everyone to meet together. During an initial IFSP meeting, introductions are vital, and this is an ideal time to decide on preferred methods of communication, as highlighted earlier. Meetings to review and revise the IFSP goals and outcomes are typically held every six months, but they can be requested at any other time (IDEA 2004). The IFSP meeting is where family-centered functional outcomes are determined; therefore, all team members should be present and asked for input during this meeting. With parental consent, early childhood educators can be present at the IFSP meeting. They have essential information regarding the child's skills, strengths, and areas of concern in the classroom and with peers. If an outcome listed on the IFSP is no longer appropriate, a meeting can be convened to revise the IFSP.

Gathering and Using Data

Initially, Genevieve is concerned about the amount of time it will take her to collect data related to Alex's outcomes. She wants to find ways to authentically collect data within her setting. For example, Alex has outcomes related to participating in parallel play during structured and unstructured play time in familiar settings. He also has outcomes related to identifying basic emotions (happy, sad, angry, and so on) when looking at books or playing. Genevieve and Tyra work together to create a data sheet for the target behaviors so that any adult in the classroom can easily and quickly fill it out. With these sheets available, Genevieve has data by the end of each day on Alex's play, social, emotional, and communication behaviors related to his outcomes.

Within the home setting, Tyra talks with Alex's family to learn about their nurturing and responsive parenting practices to help increase Alex's emotion regulation. The family is also encouraged to openly validate Alex's experiences and label his emotions throughout the day. During each visit, Tyra, Audrey, and Xavier discuss the priority for the week and how they will keep data. Some weeks, Audrey and Xavier write a brief note at the end of each day related to how Alex responded to stressful or new situations. Other weeks, they keep track of how many times Alex was able to identify emotions in books that they read each day. Audrey and Xavier share this information with the rest of the team in the communication notebook.

Because each team member collects and shares data about Alex's outcomes, this information can be used to compare his behaviors across settings and to help inform service delivery.

Family-identified outcomes are a key component of the IFSP document. As such, everyone on a child's team works toward meeting these specified goals, and collecting data across settings is critical. Such information helps to guide service delivery, demonstrate that the child is making progress toward their IFSP goals and outcomes, and determine how a child is responding to interventions.

Each team member should communicate early on about effective ways to gather data for their settings and purposes. Within an early childhood setting, educators can use anecdotal notes, running records, rating scales, or frequency counts (Bates, Schenck, & Hoover 2019; Classen & Cheatham 2015; Love, Horn, & An 2019). Teams should decide on the best mechanism for collecting and sharing data that will be easy, useful, and lead to information about progress toward identified outcomes. (For an example of a data recording sheet created for use in an early learning setting, visit NAEYC.org/books/focus-infants-toddlers.)

Resources for Professionals and Families

> "Policy Statement on Inclusion of Children with Disabilities in Early Childhood Programs." Policy statement provides strategies and information for state and local programs to consider when creating inclusive early childhood settings and programs. https://sites.ed.gov/idea/idea-files/policy-statement-inclusion-of-children-with-disabilities-in-early-childhood-programs

> "Early Childhood Inclusion." A joint position statement by the Division for Early Childhood of the Council for Exceptional Children (DEC) and NAEYC. This document discusses the importance of inclusion and discusses three components (access, participation, and supports) for high-quality inclusive environments. www.dec-sped.org/position-statements

> DEC Recommended Practices. This website provides many resources related to the DEC Recommended Practices, which describe what early childhood educators should include as the foundation of their work with children and families. https://dec-sped.org/recommendedpractices

> "Practice Improvement Tools: Using the DEC Recommended Practices," Early Childhood Technical Assistance Center. This webpage includes resources to use in conjunction with the Recommended Practices. The checklists provide a quick description of what a provider should do; the illustrations are short videos showing the practices in action; the practice guides provide a description of how to implement the practices. http://ectacenter.org/decrp

> "Results Matters Video Library—Just Being Kids." The videos in this collection show young children and their families collaborating with early interventionists in homes and a variety of community settings. www.cde.state.co.us/resultsmatter/RMVideoSeries_JustBeingKids

All Team Members Have a Voice

As Genevieve's year draws to a close, she marvels at the progress Alex has made. His communication skills are improving; he routinely engages in parallel play; he has even started identifying specific emotions and interacting more regularly with one or two particular children from class. Alex's team continues gathering data and meeting regularly. His family remains an involved, integral part of his team.

Genevieve recalls how uncertain she was when the year began. As a new teacher, she doubted her classroom expertise and underestimated the value her voice and observations would have amid a much more experienced group of professionals. Now, she sees the integral role she played in Alex's progress. Thanks to the team's collaboration and the ongoing and consistent communication among all of its members, she ends the year knowing that she is armed with tools and support that will guide her in shaping the lives and outcomes of future students.

Many effective strategies can be used when educating and caring for infants and toddlers with delays or disabilities in a variety of inclusive settings. Optimal teaming relies on shared responsibility among early interventionists, early childhood educators, administrators, and families. All team members should reach out to one another to appropriately support the child across daily routines and activities. All team members have a voice; when in doubt, reach out!

CHRISTINE M. SPENCE, PhD, is an associate professor of special education at Virginia Commonwealth University, program faculty for Virginia Leadership Education in Neurodevelopmental Disabilities (LEND), and program coordinator for the early childhood special education BSEd and MEd programs.

DESERAI MILLER, PhD, LCSW, is an instructor at the University of Illinois, Urbana-Champaign.

CATHERINE CORR, PhD, is an associate professor in the Department of Special Education at the University of Illinois, Urbana-Champaign.

ROSA MILAGROS SANTOS, PhD, is the associate provost for faculty development at the University of Illinois, Urbana-Champaign, providing leadership with processes and policies. She is also a full professor in the Department of Special Education.

BRANDIE BENTLEY, PhD, is a postdoctoral research fellow at Michigan Medicine in Ann Arbor. Her research interests surround maternal and infant health with a focus on intersections of race, ethnicity, and disability.

CHAPTER 21

Exploring Outdoors
First Learning Experiences in Nature

Mary Benson McMullen and Dylan Brody

The best place for infants to experience the natural world is to be in it—outdoors! Young infants first experience nature and the wider world around them while in the arms of the caring adults in their lives. All children, even young infants, must have time outdoors, whether that time is spent in an outdoor play yard, on a patio or deck, or during a buggy or stroller walk. As long as they are dressed appropriately for the weather and sunscreen covers all exposed skin, children benefit from being outdoors. They begin to form their first conceptions of nature from feeling the sun and breeze on their skin, seeing puffy clouds swirling overhead, smelling newly cut grass and flowers blooming, and hearing the sounds of birds chirping nearby. They will delight in exploring blades of grass and dandelions, the texture of the dirt or sand, or the crunchiness of fallen leaves around them.

Being Attuned to Young Infants

When introducing young infants to nature and the natural world, look for their communication cues, such as signs that a child is relaxed, frightened, or becoming overstimulated. The goal is to help young infants develop a positive relationship with and appreciation for nature, so do your best to help them have positive experiences with the natural world.

You can facilitate infants' social and emotional learning and development when outdoors through shared experiences, primarily through conversation (Fox 2016; Veselack, Miller, & Cain-Chang 2015). Consider the following example of a teacher enjoying a buggy ride experience with young infants:

> "The sun feels so warm! Doesn't it, friends?" Mr. Iroh says to a small group of infants during their daily walk. "I love the gentle breeze; it will keep us

from getting too hot. Do you feel it on your skin? Oh, Jade, I see the breeze is blowing your hat. Let me tie it to your chin so it doesn't blow away."

A little farther down the path, he continues, "Did you hear something, Luis? Let's all listen. What is it? Oh, I see; I think it's a bunch of birds making all that noise. Do you all hear that? It sounds a bit like . . ." Mr. Iroh imitates a squawking noise, and the children babble and coo in response. "You think that's funny?" He squawks again. "Oh my! Just look at the birds, they're all taking off and flying away together, way up high in the sky!" he says while raising his hands up in the air. "I wonder why. Where are they going?"

"What are you looking at, Seraphina? What do you see?" he asks. "Oh, look, everyone. Seraphina spotted two squirrels racing each other up that big tree where the birds were!" Mr. Iroh draws the children's attention toward the tree. "Around and around they go! I wonder, do you think it was the squirrels that scared the birds and made them fly away?"

Although this teacher is the only one speaking in this example, it is not simple chatter—it is a back-and-forth conversation. He knows the children well and responds to cues from individual children. By paying careful attention to facial expressions, body language, and the early vocalizations of the young infants, the teacher observes what drew the interest of individual children and comments on those specific things. The teacher speaks to the children in a natural tone as he names objects, provides context, uses vivid descriptors, and models observation skills and curiosity. He shares his feelings of wonder and joy in their communal encounter with nature.

Remember also the value of silence and to sometimes let nature speak for itself. Quiet moments outdoors are just as important to a young infant's development of a positive relationship with the natural world as conversations. It is in moments of quiet, of stillness, that children have the opportunity to learn to listen with their hearts and experience the sense of contentment that can be felt from just being in nature.

Rich Outdoor Play for Learning

Ellen Veselack, director of the preschool program and associate director for the Outdoor Classroom Project at the Child Educational Center in La Cañada, California, provides the reflection below about supporting cognitive development, learning, and well-being in very young children:

At the Child Educational Center, we have a strong focus on our outdoor classrooms, and we take even the very youngest children outdoors on a daily basis. There is no better way for children to gain important cognitive skills, including executive function skills, than in a nature-filled space. We have very little in the way of plastic or manufactured materials in our infant and toddler spaces, indoors or outdoors. When children interact with the natural world—and the natural world is incorporated into many different spaces—they begin to understand a number of cognitive skills, such as spatial relationships, classification, a sense of quantity and size, geometry, cause and effect, and creativity and imagination.

All children, but especially very young infants, experience the world through their senses. They sense the elements around them aided by items such as wind chimes and spinners that come alive in a breeze. That same breeze rustles the leaves in the trees, provoking children to stare up into the branches. Birds twittering from a nearby branch create another provocation. Weather events, such as rain, offer opportunities not available indoors. The smell of the wet earth, the feel of the damp air, and the shimmer of the rain on the grass all give infants new information to process. Toddlers also love a good puddle for stomping in and mud to explore!

We carefully select natural materials that are safe for very young children to engage with and explore. Items such as stumps, logs, branches, leaves, pine cones, larger stones and shells, tree rounds, seedpods, and a variety of nontoxic plants all provide endless open-ended opportunities for infants and toddlers. These items become pretend food, telephones to talk on, or just items to fill baskets, boxes, and purses.

While much of our environment is full of nature, not everything can come from nature. There are the important three *B*s of toys—books, baby dolls, and boxes. Books are everywhere for children, both indoors and out, and always available for children to pick out, pick up, look at by themselves, be read to, and even to explore orally (that is what young infants do, after all). Baby dolls are also important for children to role play and reenact family life. Infants and toddlers are drawn to baby dolls and already understand caring tenderly for them. They wrap them up in blankets, feed them with a pine cone bottle, and rock them to sleep. Toddlers, in particular, have a great affinity for boxes. They climb in and out of them, pile into them together, and play hide-and-seek in them. They push them up and down the sidewalk. They fill them with leaves and then dump them out again.

A good rule of thumb for play materials for infants and toddlers is the less the toy does (minimal need for batteries, bells, and whistles) and the more natural it is, the richer the play will be.

Discovery with Mobile Infants

Because mobile infants discover new things using all of their senses, direct encounters with nature and natural items need to be carefully planned and supervised. As they learn to move about more freely, it is important for you to be extra cautious about their safety while providing access to interesting discoveries in their environment. With the increasing ability to participate in joint or shared attention with you or a peer comes an important social development: drawing attention to what they want another person to look at by pointing at it or using some other, primarily nonverbal means. Mobile infants can engage socially in an experience or activity in a way they could not before.

Conclusion

Exploring and being in nature is invaluable not only because it is a gateway to learning about things like biology, geology, or ecology, but also because it opens doors to our understanding of ourselves and our place within the world (Bruce 2021; Tovey 2020). Forming a positive relationship with the natural world and

living things early in life impacts lifetime notions of who we are as social beings, how we see ourselves in relation to others, and what it means to care for and be compassionate about others and the world around us (Thompson & Thompson 2007). Appreciating nature and feeling joyful and content when in nature sustains our emotional well-being and is at the very heart and soul of defining who we are and who we become as human beings (Louv 2008; Rivkin 2014).

MARY BENSON McMULLEN, PhD, is professor of early childhood education at Indiana University, where she has been on faculty since 1993. Her numerous publications include articles, book chapters, and books for researchers and education professionals.

DYLAN BRODY, MSED, is a doctoral candidate at the University of Georgia. They are currently a graduate research assistant for the Department of Educational Theory and Practice, with a focus on critical studies.

Using the Environment and Materials as Curriculum for Promoting Exploration of Cause and Effect

Guadalupe Rivas Jer

I work at a campus-based center that provides children with an emergent, child-centered, play-based curriculum to support their natural curiosity and exploration within a safe, supportive, and nurturing environment. My colleagues and I thoughtfully plan play spaces and experiences that support curricular goals based on infants' and toddlers' play interests and talents "through both pre-planned, teacher-directed, intentional activities, and child-initiated, emerging play activities" (Shin & Partyka 2017, 127). This chapter reflects the integration of developmentally appropriate materials and opportunities for infant exploration and how a curriculum is influenced by educators' planning and in-the-moment decision making.

Observing an Infant and Offering Choices

At almost 1 year of age, Andy stands on his own but is not walking yet. I notice that he is starting to throw toys and other objects and watch as they land on the floor. Andy will throw objects from the top of the infant loft and roll them down the loft ramp. When he is standing, he will pick up an object and raise his arm to throw it, and sometimes the object will land on a peer. I want to provide Andy with additional, safer ways to explore cause-and-effect relationships.

The dramatic play/block area in the infant classroom has a long see-through plastic tube fastened to the wall so that it is elevated at one end to make an incline (see the photo). We put the tube in this fixed position so that children can put materials inside it and see what

happens: Which ones fit in the tube? Which ones don't fit? In which end of the tube should you try to put an object if you want it to move through the tube? Which objects move through the tube? Which objects don't? Some objects slide, some objects roll. Some objects need a push, some objects don't.

I want to encourage Andy to roll wooden cars inside and down the tube to support his understanding of cause and effect and to give Andy an opportunity to continue to build his trust in me by interacting with him one-on-one. I place a car inside the tube, and

Andy watches as it slides down and exits the other end. "Bye-bye, car," I say as the car rolls down. Andy crawls to the end of the tube and picks up the car. He places it on the bottom of the tube, but it rolls back down almost immediately since it has only a short distance to roll. I say, "Andy, look!" and roll another car from the top of the tube. Andy picks it up and puts the car in the space between the tube and the wall. He laughs and looks at me. I clap, smile, and say, "Yay!"

A few days later, I notice Andy standing in front of the clear tube holding a car. It is the first time he appears interested in the tube without my prompting. He holds the car in his left hand (his nondominant hand) and places it in the tube, but he seems to have a hard time opening his hand in the tube so he can let the car go. He pulls out his hand and tries again. Andy furrows his brow and babbles. I ask, "Andy, are you frustrated because the car isn't going in the tube?" He looks at me and babbles some more. Wondering if it might be easier for Andy to let go of the car if he uses his dominant hand, I encourage him. "Try again. Try your other hand." Andy looks up at me but does not respond to this suggestion. After a few more tries, Andy is able to put the car in the tube and let go of it, but it gets stuck because the car is on its side. Andy puts his whole hand through to push the car, and the car goes halfway down. "Yay! Andy, you did it! You pushed the car through!" I say enthusiastically. Even though the car did not roll all the way down, I still celebrate Andy's efforts to explore cause and effect by manipulating the car so it would fit into the tube.

The following week, I notice that the children are becoming more interested in balls. I decide to focus the curriculum on balls and tie that focus to Andy's interest in the tube. I have only soft balls and bouncy balls the size of a volleyball, so I order some smaller plastic balls that fit inside the tube. I think Andy will have an easier time rolling the balls than the cars, though he will still have the choice of both materials. I hope that Andy will feel successful if he can place the ball inside and watch it roll all the way down. This might keep up his motivation to try the cars again and to make a further cause-and-effect connection.

The following week, I invite Andy back to the tube to see if he prefers a ball or car to roll down the tube. I wonder if he has made the developmental connection that rolling the ball is not as challenging as setting the car on its wheels in the tube to roll down. I also wonder if he knows that rolling the ball in the tube always has the same results.

I offer Andy the car first, and he tries to place the car inside the tube. When he can't, he tries it with his other hand. Although I think that Andy might be able to open his hand on the first try and let go of the car if he uses his dominant hand, this does not seem to be the case. He is also still working on understanding that the car needs to be on its wheels when he lets go to make the car roll down the tube. Eventually, Andy throws the car on the ground, and I offer the car and ball to him. He takes the car but then drops it to pick up the ball. He places the ball into the elevated end of the tube and watches it roll down the tube. About three weeks has elapsed since I first introduced Andy to the tube. After this, when given the option between the ball and the car, Andy almost always chooses the ball.

> **DAP** Identifying specific learning goals for infants and toddlers aids in the planning and preparation of play spaces and materials. Teachers identify specific language and thinking skills to introduce and encourage during play.

Reflections on Andy's Experiences

As I noticed and responded to Andy's increasing curiosity about the effect of his actions on objects and materials, I offered different opportunities and materials to scaffold his understanding of cause and effect. He explored the physical properties of the long, clear tube by placing cars and balls inside it. Reading Andy's social and visual cues, and offering guidance only as he needed it, I used oral and nonverbal language to scaffold his exploration of the tube and how objects move through it.

During the initial tube interaction, Andy didn't seem to understand that placing materials at the top of the tunnel makes them slide down to the other end. When he showed signs of frustration, I provided responsive caregiving—an example of "sensitivity to children's movements, sounds, and gestures and interpreting and responding appropriately to them" (Lucas, Richter, & Daelmans 2018, 42). While I continued to invite Andy to experiment with objects in the tube, eventually he explored it on his own. I used Andy's interest in things that move and in cause and effect to strengthen his cognitive, physical, self-regulation, and relationship skills.

Extending the Exploration with All Children

We extended this activity by reading books about objects that roll and move, singing and moving to songs about emotions, and writing a social story about Andy's tube exploration for his family. We also provided Andy and the children with different-sized materials to help them differentiate between objects that fit or don't fit into the tube and build on each of their actions, thereby extending the curricular play and exploration around the beginning stages of classification.

As often happens in emergent curriculum planning for infants and toddlers, we do not expect to create a month's curriculum on cause and effect for a whole group of children based on one child's interest. Throughout the month, the children rolled balls down an open ramp and through a tunnel ramp; participated in water sensory activities and hit water with their palms, causing the water to splash; created music by shaking rattles and hitting notes on a xylophone; and used a sticky wall to stick materials to it and pull them off. All of these activities were planned in response to observing, interacting, and responding to children's exploration and curiosity. We planned extended activities that would integrate self-regulation, language, cognitive, and social competencies for the children. This approach requires teachers to interact closely with infants and toddlers to inform meaningful and developmentally appropriate curriculum planning and implementation. "The children are the curriculum. Objective and detailed observation of the children's desires, activity choices, interests, passions, and challenges will provide educators with all the curriculum they will ever need" (Murphy 2016, 28).

GUADALUPE RIVAS JER, MA, works as a California state preschool project specialist for the San Mateo County Office of Education. She holds a master's degree in early childhood education from San Francisco State University.

CHAPTER 23

Infant and Toddler STEAM

Supporting Interdisciplinary Experiences with Our Youngest Learners

Eric Bucher and Stephanie Pindra

How do science, technology, engineering, arts, and mathematics (STEAM) relate to infants and toddlers? This chapter shares ways teachers can support the development of infants' and toddlers' STEAM-related skills, make connections between children's interests and intentional teaching practices, and create spaces that promote developmentally appropriate STEAM learning.

Starting with what is known about child development, let's reflect on how young children from infancy to kindergarten engage with learning:

> Curious about what she sees, 9-month-old Emilia scoots toward a flicker of sunlight glimmering from a reflective decoration on the window. She reaches her hand out to try and touch it. She turns her hand around in the flashing light. She clenches her fist a few times and looks up at her teacher, who is observing closely nearby. Emilia furrows her brow as if silently asking about what is happening. Her teacher responds, "It looks like you noticed the light reflecting. Are you trying to catch it, I wonder?"

· · · · · · · · · · · · ·

> Two-year-old Alfonso goes immediately to the large cardboard container boxes that his father has placed on the living room carpet for him to explore. Alfonso stacks them as high as he is tall. As he reaches to place another box on top, the stack topples over. Alfonso pauses, and then points and giggles, "Fall down." His father replies, "Gravity!" Alfonso stacks the blocks again. This time, he swipes his hand against the middle and down the boxes fall. Alfonso laughs again and says, "It fall down!" His father encourages him to continue building, deconstructing, and testing out his theories.

· · · · · · · · · · · · ·

> Marcus and Sherice, both 5 years old, are investigating the natural desert items displayed on a mirror on an outside table. The teacher has taken time to prepare a variety of natural objects, watercolor paint, permanent markers, and clipboards with paper outdoors as a provocation for children to engage in artistic representation. Sherice chooses to use a magnifying glass to look at the details of a delicate flower more closely before sketching her observations. She uses watercolors to try to capture the hues she sees. Marcus explains to Sherice that he is helping her mix colors to make a shade of red that matches the flower.

All of these examples reveal children's emerging theories about the world and how they can interact with it. Children are active, competent, and engaged learners. Their learning occurs in the context of relationships with materials and with a nurturing caregiver who is attuned to the child's strengths and interests.

For infants and toddlers, the exploration of STEAM is part of the development of lifelong learning skills in cognitive development and approaches to learning. Early STEAM experiences help develop wonder, persistence, communication, problem solving, and mental flexibility. Development of these skills depends on a child's developmental abilities and interests, their access to stimulating open-ended materials, and on the extent to which they have a caring, responsive, and secure relationship with their caregiver (Bredekamp & Willer 2022).

In the preschool years, children exhibit STEAM skills in a variety of ways. They may use different tools or materials to investigate natural items in their outdoor learning space, identify cause-and-effect relationships with ramps and pathways in the block center, or represent their ideas through art materials offered in the writing center. Developing foundational learning behaviors in early learning experiences, such as risk taking in exploration, close observation, hypothesis formation, analysis based on evidence, and communication, set the stage for further learning when children enter kindergarten.

What Does STEAM Look Like in Infant and Toddler Development?

Infants and toddlers are young scientists conducting research to find out how the world works. They are curious to figure things out, like whether they will get the same result when they drop a toy—and have you pick it up—over and over. Infants and toddlers understand concepts such as cause and effect that help them build sophisticated reasoning skills and conceptual knowledge (Bucher & Hernández 2016; NASEM 2022; USDHHS 2015).

For example, a 2-year-old might roll a ball down a slide to observe what happens. Then the toddler might retrieve the ball and test it out again. If the ball repeatedly bounces underneath the slide, disappearing from view, the child may exhibit problem-solving skills by changing their movement or rolling the ball up the slide instead, adjusting their approach based on what they see happen. These careful observations of flexibility in thinking show the toddler's growing understanding of cause and effect and of the properties of materials. When paired with a sense of curiosity to explore and a teacher's openness to supporting these types of experiences, infants and toddlers start to figure out how things work and how they can use their bodies to make things happen.

Infants' and toddlers' cognitive skills and approaches to learning are made visible through their interactions as well as through their verbal communication. This requires teachers to observe children closely to pick up on cues about what interests them and what ideas they may be testing. Infants and toddlers use many expressive nonverbal forms of communication

through which teachers can come to discern their interests, curiosities, approaches, and hypotheses. These observable actions—smiles, hand and body movements, gestures, mimicry, eyebrow furrows, and eye focus—reveal children's understandings of the world (Gambetti & Gandini 2014). "Infant and Toddler Approaches to Learning/Cognitive Development," on page 111, shows several developmental skills and observable actions related to infants' and toddlers' STEAM learning (USDHHS 2015).

Supporting STEAM Engagement with Infants and Toddlers

Learning happens best within the context of safe, secure, positive relationships (Iruka 2022; NRC 2015). Through a learning environment that values and actively supports healthy relationships, educators provide joyful play experiences that engage children in exploring STEAM knowledge and skills. The following strategies build nurturing relationships and enrich learning environments for infants and toddlers:

> **Respect children as capable and competent learners.** Young children are capable of observing, interacting, and building hypotheses about the world. By carefully focusing on children's actions, teachers notice all the ways children are intentional, competent, and have their own ideas.

> **Set up an environment that supports joy, curiosity, and engagement.** Viewing themselves as STEAM researchers, teachers engage in collaborative dialogue with other teachers and reflect on their teaching practice (Marsh & Gonzalez 2018; Newman & Woodrow 2015; Schroeder Yu 2012). At times, teachers step back and allow infants and toddlers to explore with minimal intervention. This allows teachers to understand the way the children engage and investigate and influences their selection of

Infant and Toddler Approaches to Learning/Cognitive Development Related to STEAM

Developmental Skills	Observable Infant and Toddler Behaviors
Executive function	■ Persists ■ Develops confidence ■ Approaches new experiences and takes risks ■ Maintains focus and sustains attention
Initiative and curiosity	■ Shows eagerness and curiosity as a learner ■ Initiates actions with materials
Creativity and inventiveness	■ Experiments with different uses for objects ■ Is flexible in actions and behavior
Exploration and discovery	■ Uses senses to explore ■ Observes ■ Makes things happen, watches for results, repeats ■ Uses understanding of causal relationships
Memory	■ Recalls and uses information in new situations
Reasoning and problem solving	■ Uses a variety of strategies, imagination, and creativity to solve problems ■ Uses spatial awareness to understand properties of objects and their movement in space ■ Applies knowledge to new situations

instructional strategies and approaches to further support children's interests and understandings (Reggio Children 2016).

> **Observe and document children's interests and skills.** To capture evidence of STEAM skills, teachers observe and document children's interactions by taking photos, recording anecdotal notes, and reflecting on their observations (Abramson 2012). Teachers listen, observe, reflect, research, and develop activities based on what they notice over time. They use their reflective study of documentation to organize thoughts as a method to look at what children are doing and to meet the children where they are (Carter & Curtis 2017).

> **Offer interesting materials and experiences to promote problem solving, creativity, and persistence.** Even very young children can engage for long periods of time when materials spark wonder and curiosity and when adult support is nurturing and intentional (Curtis & Carter 2015). Infants and toddlers are captivated by looking at and touching fresh flowers, translucent materials, and recycled pieces on a light table; building, stacking, and sitting in boxes; filling and dumping containers; and scooping and pouring sand and water.

Resources for Supporting STEAM with Infants and Toddlers

Age	Developmentally Appropriate Materials	What Educators and Children Can Do Together	Vocabulary to Include in Conversation
Birth to 9 months	Mirror on the floor for looking at or crawling over Pots, pans, wooden spoons, and unbreakable bowls Recycled materials made from plastic or metal Reflective materials near windows/light sources	Offer materials that support children to try a variety of movements (grasp, pinch, roll, squeeze, turn around, mouth, chew). Hold infants closely in lap and point out pictures in books while reading together. Model observation skills: "I notice you are interested in using your hand to tap the top of the pots. It makes a metal ringing sound!" Place interesting objects just out of reach so infants problem solve their movement.	*Approach* *Explore* *Learning* *Notice* *Curious*: "You are a curious researcher!" Describe the child's actions using interesting verbs: "I see you stretching to reach that toy. Just a little bit farther!"
8 to 18 months	Various shapes, sizes, and types of cardboard boxes Recycled materials made from plastic or metal Light table with interesting transparent objects	Scaffold children to be challenged based on their skills by offering questions: "I wonder what you can do with this?" "What do you notice?" Set up a space where children can engage in light and shadow play. The light table may include interesting objects from the child's home and culture.	*Observe* *Problem solving/ problem solver* *Persist*: "I can see that you are persisting to try to solve that problem."
16 to 36 months	Sand or water with various measuring, stirring, and sifting tools Rubber balls and open spaces for rolling Stackable or connectable items like cardboard boxes and blocks	Place out materials and tools with which toddlers can scoop, pour, fill, and repeat with varying movements. Encourage children to construct and deconstruct materials (e.g., building up and knocking down) by describing what you observe about cause and effect.	*Reasoning* *Test* *Think* *Understand* *Research* Describe the child's actions using interesting verbs: "You are filling the bucket full of water. Now, it's spilling out. Do you want to measure more water into the bucket?"

> **Plan for intentional interactions.** Building on children's interests and the evidence of their current abilities and understandings can be done intentionally. Try these strategies:

- Ask open-ended questions like "What do you notice?" "Why do you think that happened?" and "What are you thinking about?"

- Provide new and interesting developmentally appropriate materials for children to investigate. Place child-safe mirrors on the floor for an infant's tummy time or offer a basket of recycled materials like paper towel tubes and empty containers to toddlers outside. Offer variations of materials that infants and toddlers enjoy, such as smaller boxes to add on to large cardboard boxes or larger wrapping paper tubes that can be used as ramps or tunnels.

- Model vocabulary and conversations during your interactions with children. Describe the green color of paint a toddler mixed as matching steamed broccoli, or use phrases like "I think . . ." and "I wonder . . . " or narrate a child's actions during diaper changing (La Paro, Hamre, & Pianta 2007).

intentional observation and documentation strategies, and approach their teaching with curiosity, they can enhance infant and toddler STEAM learning.

ERIC BUCHER, EdD, is a research assistant professor of early childhood policy at the Children's Equity Project at Arizona State University.

STEPHANIE PINDRA has been an Early Head Start teacher in New Mexico and Arizona and has worked with extraordinary toddlers for more than 20 years.

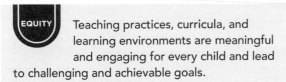

EQUITY — Teaching practices, curricula, and learning environments are meaningful and engaging for every child and lead to challenging and achievable goals.

"Resources for Supporting STEAM with Infants and Toddlers," on page 112, offers additional ideas for materials and interactions that support infants' and toddlers' STEAM learning.

Conclusion

For infants and toddlers, STEAM experiences support the development of essential cognitive skills and approaches to learning—like problem solving, persistence, creativity, and reasoning—that are crucial to engaged and joyful learning and that serve as the foundation for more complex understanding of STEAM content as children grow older. When teachers provide safe and secure relationships, practice

PART 6

Demonstrating Professionalism as an Early Childhood Educator

RECOMMENDATIONS FROM THE DAP STATEMENT

Developmentally appropriate practice serves as the hallmark of the early childhood education profession. Fully achieving its guidelines and effectively promoting all young children's development and learning depends on the establishment of a strong profession with which all early childhood educators, working across all settings, identify. Educators use the guidelines of the profession, including these guidelines, as they conduct themselves as members of the profession and serve as informed advocates for young children and their families as well as the profession itself.

Reyna's two children enrolled at Learning Time Children's Place six months after she and her family immigrated to the United States from the Philippines. The program became the source of lasting friendships and stability for her family. Reyna joined the parent board and often spent time in the classroom with her daughters. When a position for a classroom aide opened, she eagerly took it. While she held a college degree from the Philippines, she needed to add nine credits of early childhood coursework to earn the required early childhood credential. With the help of a scholarship, she enrolled in the local community college. Over the next five years, she achieved a teaching credential.

With the support of her director, Reyna became a member of NAEYC and her state Affiliate, attending annual conferences and developing a greater sense of commitment to the profession. When invited to go with a group of professionals to talk with the mayor about the importance of early childhood programs in the community and opportunities for collaboration and funding, she went along. The next fall, when the same group traveled to the state capital to talk with members of Congress, she

was determined and confident. Reyna shared her personal journey as a single mother and the impact of high-quality education for her daughters and the children she taught.

As you consider your own professional journey so far, what have you learned that makes you feel confident as an educator? What advice would you give to someone else just beginning? What struggles and challenges have you experienced? What other experiences and skills would help you be more successful in your work? Developmentally appropriate practice includes a focus on professionalism, which means taking steps forward to develop new skills and participate more fully in the field of early childhood education.

The profession of early childhood includes the aligned network of people dedicated to promoting children's optimal development, including educators, families, and specialists and the community, education, social, and political systems that surround and support the profession. It includes the ways educators connect with families and make the most of resources in the community. It also includes the important work of advocating for yourself, for families and children, and for the systems that support high-quality early childhood education.

As you think about what professionalism means to you, perhaps you remember a mentor who encouraged you to grow in your understanding or experience. Maybe you think about the steps you took to attend a conference, enroll in early childhood coursework, or pursue a degree. The journey of professional advancement will lead you to seek opportunities outside of your program to help you grow.

At the same time, opportunities to grow as a professional exist within your program. Professionalism requires a commitment to developmentally appropriate practice and developing the skills and practices needed for high-quality teaching. This work depends on reflective and intentional practice to address increasingly complex issues in teaching and with understanding of diverse communities of families and children to inform decision making. Perhaps you have invited colleagues to join you at a conference or help you organize a community of practice. Collaboration with colleagues can help you examine ways of thinking and develop greater sensitivity to the experiences and contexts of others. Together, you will develop new strengths, explore opportunities to grow and learn, and identify resources to help you advance your practice.

Another important step is active participation as a member of the early childhood profession. As you explore the NAEYC position statements, ethical guidelines, standards, and other resources, what you learn will strengthen your practice. In addition, you will gain new skills to become an informed and active advocate for young children, families, your program, and the profession. You will learn more about current trends and issues that impact the profession as a whole, including local, state, and national policies.

In Part 6, you'll see a few of the ways professionalism and advocacy come together to support the practices, policies, and systems of infant and toddler teaching. You will discover the importance of each individual teacher, family, and others working together to create and sustain high-quality, accessible early learning experiences for all children.

Learning Stories to learn about and from children? Who will you bring together to reflect on and discuss children's experiences?

"Thinking of Yourself as a Professional" offers a professional perspective about the need for advocacy as an essential part of the early childhood professional journey. It highlights the importance of sharing personal stories as a foundation for advocacy. **Consider:** What is the story of your professional journey? How did you become an early childhood educator? What steps do you want to take so that others can benefit from hearing your story?

"Advocacy in Action: Stepping Up to Make an Impact" addresses the pressing challenges of teacher preparation, the wage gap, staffing, and diversity. The author calls for early childhood professionals to become advocates, with strategies to create positive change at the local, state, and national levels. **Consider:** What are some first steps you can take to share your experiences in the field with others? Research opportunities to attend local and state events and brainstorm with colleagues how to more actively advocate for early childhood policies that benefit children, families, and educators.

READ AND REFLECT

As you read the chapters in this section, consider and evaluate your own classroom practices using these reflection questions.

"Nurturing Your Professional Appetite: Preparing Your Professional Development Path" shows how educators can explore a range of professional development options and advance their growth journey. **Consider:** Think about the people and organizations that are part of your professional network. What are your professional interests and goals? What types of opportunities might be available to you? How could you advocate for more opportunities?

"Creating Learning Stories in the Context of Inquiry Groups" demonstrates the transforming professional development processes of teacher inquiry, documentation, and reflection as vital means of growth and effectiveness in teaching. Educators engage in the creation of Learning Stories to observe and document children's learning using a strengths-based approach; this authentic, shared process becomes the basis of collaboration and planning with colleagues and families. **Consider:** How can Learning Stories bring together staff and families to reflect a rich, comprehensive picture of children's development? How can you use

NEXT STEPS

After reading Part 6, consider the following suggestions as you plan next steps in your own professional journey.

1. What have you already accomplished or achieved that makes you feel proud to be an early childhood professional? Describe the obstacles that have challenged you, and what dispositions, skills, and action steps you took to overcome them.

2. Which people and resources have helped you during your professional journey, and what additional resources do you want to make use of as you move forward? What colleagues can you invite to share that journey with you?

3. Take time to think about your own personal story and what that can mean to others. What inspires you to become more active in advocacy with and on behalf of families and children? What next steps would you like to take to advance your professional journey of advocacy?

References for the chapters in this part can be accessed online at NAEYC.org/books/focus-infants-toddlers.

CHAPTER 24

Nurturing Your Professional Appetite

Preparing Your Professional Development Path

Christy Brown-John

During my first days of teaching at a university laboratory school with young toddlers, I was fortunate enough to develop a lasting relationship with the master teacher with whom I worked. At that time, I didn't have experience working in child care, certainly not with infants and toddlers, and I had no real working knowledge of child development. I found myself learning more about "how" to teach children rather than "what" to teach, and it changed my whole perspective about what I was being called to do. I became a student, and the children became my educators. It gave new meaning to the term *lifelong learner,* and I was able to embrace this idea in a way I hadn't known before. I came to realize that what I knew wasn't enough, and I needed to look for more learning opportunities. Those learning opportunities helped guide my career, and I became a coach and trainer for infant and toddler professionals working in center- and home-based child care settings. My colleague played a critical role in my professional journey.

Later in my training career, as I was unpacking my car and preparing to begin a training session, I overheard the group of infant and toddler educators who would be in the session talking to one another. One professional said, "Why are we even here today? I need to clean and organize my classroom." Others said, "We've heard this before; we're not going to learn anything" and "How do they expect us to learn this new curriculum? We don't have time to add one more thing to our day." I realized these professionals needed a menu of options so they could choose the content and learning formats that meet their own needs and not leave them feeling uninvested or overwhelmed.

There are many types of professional learning formats you can use to satisfy your desire to learn more about child development or increase the quality of care in your program. How do you know which opportunity is right for you? Is one better than another? Wouldn't it be great if you had a menu to choose the ones that work best for you?

If you are hungry to improve your practice but unsure where to begin, there is a rich menu of options that you can choose from to create a professional learning plan just right for you.

Selecting Appetizers

A learning appetizer is a small, bite-sized option for professional growth and learning. You can have as many as you like, as they are served in small enough portions to fit with your interests and schedule. Here are some great ways to get started:

> **Social support.** Supervisors, coworkers, and fellow educators can be a great source for professional learning. They may share ideas, activities, or have recommendations of strategies to increase your professional knowledge of working with infants and toddlers. Sometimes you just need someone to listen to your struggles as you discover the best solution to your problem on your own. Coworkers can serve as peer mentors and supervisors can often impart wisdom from lessons they've learned from experience.

> **Communities of practice and professional learning communities.** Shared learning experiences can be valuable to infant and toddler

educators because they take place in a community made up of colleagues who face similar professional situations. These groups often create their discussion topics based on the expressed needs of the members, which makes learning relevant and meaningful.

> **Professional organizations.** NAEYC, the National Association for Family Child Care (NAFCC), and Zero to Three are organizations known nationally that offer a variety of benefits for infant and toddler educators. Joining a professional organization that recognizes the value of the early care and education community is a solid place to start for infant and toddler educators interested in increasing their knowledge, skills, and professionalism. When you become an active member, you are part of a larger community of like-minded professionals who understand the value of the work you do. These professional organizations provide opportunities to expand your social support network beyond your coworkers and geographical neighbors.

> **Social media.** NAEYC offers interest forums as well as an online community that connect through the online platform HELLO. Conversations are also held over various social media platforms, like Twitter, Facebook, and LinkedIn. You can also use your own private social media account and group pages to connect to other professionals. Social media is a great platform to crowdsource information. For example, you can share ideas and resources, seek help with current challenges, and celebrate successes you have experienced.

> **Professional resources.** Maybe you have searched the internet to learn more about how to soothe a fussy baby or scrolled through social media for engaging toddler activities. No doubt you have come across ideas that you tried. Perhaps you stumbled across new art experiences that look exciting. While those resources may be helpful, be sure you have a critical eye when it comes to bringing those new practices into your high-quality infant or toddler classroom. A professional educator will consider how any activity or experience supports the learning and development milestones infants and toddlers are working toward. Resources that have been researched, peer reviewed, or proven effective through evidence-based methods allow you to introduce materials or practice newly acquired skills with confidence. Books produced by trusted early education publishers, journals published through a peer review process, and articles grounded in evidence-based research are good sources of content that reflects relevant and current information and offers effective teaching strategies. As you pursue these resources, do so with a critical eye, and seek sources from researchers that are diverse and experts who hold a perspective that differs from yours.

DAP Participating in a continuum of professional development opportunities equips teachers with the knowledge, skills, practices, and dispositions to make complex decisions in the classroom and work effectively with families.

Choosing a Main Course

Now that you have sampled a taste of professionalism, you should have worked up an appetite for more. It's time to consider a heartier menu item that will keep you full a bit longer. These next menu options are known as training or professional development, are widely used, and offer a variety of delivery methods. Whether you participate in person or online, live or recorded, training can be a great source of information for improving your practice.

> **Workshops and webinars.** Workshops and webinars are often referred to as single trainings that have a lot to offer the infant and toddler educator. You can fill your plate with enough trainings to make a full meal or select one to try new ideas and decide if you'd like to explore a topic a bit further. For example, you might take a training on exploring science with young children and realize the topic is exciting to you; next, you might want to learn how to incorporate science exploration within the curriculum or through everyday experiences.

> **Training series**. Training activities are often sought to fulfill a credential requirement or may provide a series of sessions over a period of time. Specialized training, such as "The Growing Brain" training series by Zero to Three, is a professional

learning experience for educators to deepen their understanding of a specific topic. You may be pursuing a certification, like a Child Development Associate (CDA) Credential. Additional topics may include preservice or orientation training, child care policies and procedures, infant and toddler curriculum, child development, or observation and assessment.

> **On-site mentoring.** A mentor once reminded me that even Olympic gold medalists have a coach to help them train and improve their skills. Research has shown that on-site coaching and mentoring is one of the most effective professional learning strategies to support educator practices when caring for children in center- or home-based child care settings (Eckhardt & Egert 2020; Reid et al. 2021). Not only is the information personalized for your child care environment, but also relationships are built between the coach and you. Opportunities for formal and self-assessment are available, and personalized feedback followed by goal setting and strategic planning are part of the coaching relationship. On-site coaching participation demonstrates your professionalism as an educator and your commitment to pursuing high-quality care and education for the infants and toddlers in your program.

Ordering Dessert

When you go out to dinner, a main course is almost always ordered. Sometimes you go for the appetizer; other times you splurge for dessert. Perhaps you need to budget for dessert in your professional life. Below are some great possibilities:

> **Family and community connections.** Connecting with families and the community as a method of professional learning is a wonderful and often underused strategy. Collaborating with community partners, such as your local librarian, community zoos and museums, early interventionists, and pediatricians offers many opportunities for an infant and toddler educator to engage in reciprocal partnerships with families while fostering community connections. For example, a family member of an infant or toddler may come to you with a particular concern regarding their child's development or behavior. Assisting them may require you to search out research or other resources. Reaching out to community partners who can offer their expertise and resources to families will provide you with the specialized knowledge needed to continue supporting the infants and toddlers in your care.

> **Professional conferences.** Explore the benefits of attending local, state, and national conferences designed for early educators like you! Professional conferences often provide access to resources, vendors, and specific topics like curriculum and help you find new products from early education businesses. Attending workshops and keynote sessions can expose you to new knowledge and expand your existing knowledge of topics and research, such as strategies for supporting social and emotional development and cognitive skills. My favorite reason for attending conferences is the energy I feel when I walk into a space that is designed for the sole purpose of connecting professionals to elevate the field of early care and education.

> **Networking.** A family child care professional I recently met shared how she followed up conference attendance by networking with professionals from other states. Those relationships benefited her personally and professionally. The groups have regularly met over the years on virtual platforms and shared resources, proving extremely helpful to her and her colleagues.

Formal education. Pursuing an advanced degree is an investment in yourself as a professional educator. Whether you seek a full degree or take a few college courses, continuing your education is a big step toward enhancing your professionalism. Community colleges provide practical courses that can lead to an associate degree. They are taught by experienced professionals who can relate to your daily life and work. University attendance opens opportunities for expanded learning and provides new ways of thinking about concepts and ideas. An advanced degree contributes to an enhanced career path that may include opportunities to train and/or coach other infant and toddler educators. National organizations and state quality initiatives are sources for scholarships and compensation support for those seeking formal education and training experiences.

positive guidance in the child care environment (Han et al. 2021). It is imperative that educators have an opportunity to create professional goals and design a learning plan that helps them support young children's development and learning (Han et al. 2021).

As you prepare your professional plate and plan your professional development path, consider the role you play, the development of the children you serve, and your own professional interests and goals. However you plan to nurture your professional appetite, make sure that it is meaningful to you and the very important work you do each day.

CHRISTY BROWN-JOHN has been working with young children and adults for more than 20 years. She currently provides professional development and learning for infant and toddler educators.

Reviewing Your Professional Development Plate

Professional development experiences support educators' ability to meet professional standards and competencies, providing opportunities for educators to pursue reflective and intentional practices as they learn and consider new and emerging research. As educators engage in continuous, collaborative learning, professional connections with peers and partnerships with community members also inform their practice.

Research shows that professional development activities like networking, coaching, collaborating with families and community members, and obtaining an advanced degree increase an educator's professionalism, reduce negative interactions between educators and children, and increase the use of

CHAPTER 25

Creating Learning Stories in the Context of Inquiry Groups

Isauro M. Escamilla, Linda R. Kroll, Daniel R. Meier, and Annie White

Teaching young children can be an overwhelming, exciting, ever-changing experience that can be the most satisfying profession. Or it can be a profession filled with frustrations, directives, and shortages. Or it can be both. Most important, teachers need to have some control and agency over their teaching and their classrooms or centers. They need to feel that they know what they are doing and why they are doing it and to feel in sync with the other teachers (in their classroom or at their program), the children, and the families who make up their learning communities. When teachers meet regularly together to reflect on what they have each noticed in their classrooms, to propose questions about what is happening, and to systematically think about what they are doing, they can feel supported in the work they do and with the children they teach and their families.

The writing of Learning Stories integrated within the professional development process of teacher inquiry, documentation, and reflection offers a new model of professional support and a method for reaching out to children and families. In this chapter, we'll consider the way Learning Stories are a natural outcome of shared inquiry learning. First, let's take a look at what Learning Stories are.

What Are Learning Stories?

Learning Stories (Carr & Lee 2012, 2019) provide a framework for teachers to observe children naturally in their learning environments and to recognize and document children's personal interests, discoveries, and talents. Learning Stories are told by educators from a strengths-based perspective, viewing the whole child as a person rather than fragmenting the child into separate parts based on predetermined assessment measures. (An example of a Learning Story appears on page 122.) The Learning Stories framework honors multiple perspectives to create more complete images of the learners, including the voices of teachers as narrators, the voices and actions of children as active participants in the learning process, and the voices of families who offer their perspective as the most important teachers in their children's lives (Escamilla, Alanís, & Meier 2023).

In using Learning Stories in classrooms and other settings, teachers enter into the intimate space of stories for children, other teachers, and families. In turn, families enter into the thinking space of teachers. When writing classroom stories where children are the protagonists of their own learning, teachers highlight their personal and community values, such as respect, collaboration, and trust, and perhaps more important, they open the door for meaningful communication with the intent to get to know and serve children better.

EQUITY Effective teachers develop the skill to observe a child's environment from the child's perspective. The process of creating Learning Stories enables educators to focus on what a child *can* do in a given context rather than what the child *isn't* doing compared with peers.

Whether you teach in a private, independent, or public early learning context, the Learning Stories approach is an effective way to observe and document small moments of learning and growth in young children with specific examples of children's questions, interests, explorations, and discoveries. The approach also allows you to document and share your own learning as a critical observer, storyteller, writer, and colleague. For teachers and leaders working in sites that use informal, cumulative assessments such as documentation panels, portfolios, and narrative notes, Learning Stories can provide an additional, complementary narrative-based form of authentic assessment.

Components and Example of a Learning Story

In a Learning Story with photographs of children engaged with materials and with peers as illustrations, teachers include these foundational paragraphs to answer the following questions:

1. What is the story? Describe what the child does and says.

2. What does it mean? Give a pedagogical analysis of the actions that took place.

3. What opportunities and possibilities arise? This refers to materials, activities, or recourses to extend the child's learning, with as much detail as possible.

4. What are the family's thoughts about their child as an engaged learner?

Learning Stories highlight developmental considerations, including children's social and emotional, physical, and linguistic growth. The events on which Azul's Learning Story (page 122) is based are described below.

Azul's Learning Story for Gael: "One, Two, Three Steps Closer"

Teacher Azul Muller presented her Learning Story, "One, Two, Three Steps Closer," to her inquiry group. It chronicled 13-month-old Gael's early attempts to walk. Azul prefaced her Learning Story by explaining that Gael was becoming the first walker in the classroom because of Azul's support and Gael's overall "perseverance and determination." Azul shared Gael's Learning Story with his mother, who asked, "Why doesn't he show me he's walking?" Azul shared the photo of Gael walking to his mother on the Monday after it happened on a Friday. Azul then sent more photographs to Gael's mother, who wanted to share them on Facebook. Because Azul's Learning Story documented Gael's first time walking in the classroom, I (author Isauro) remarked to the inquiry group that we could call it a "first-time story."

Azul told us that she planned to print out the Learning Story on larger paper and display it on the classroom wall.

Azul's story shows that learning to walk is also a social and community activity and pursuit. Azul's photographs show the close proximity of Kayla (Azul's coteacher who was with Gael) and Gael, and yet they also show how Kayla is actually not touching Gael, but has positioned her body low to the ground, with arms and hands outstretched to support Gael's efforts. Azul is the focus of Gael's walking, as he tries to reach her. Kayla's physical presence is not so much to catch Gael if he falls but to signal to Gael that she is there with him, for him, and trusts that even if he falls, he will get back up and try again as he wishes. In this sense, Kayla provides support for Gael that is as much social and emotional as physical. It is also cultural and communal, as Azul displays culturally relevant and supportive actions and language ("Hi Gael, I missed you. Do you want to sit with me? Come over") and has first written the Learning Story in Spanish, Gael's home language and the medium for Azul's initial "conversation" with Gael. In writing the story first in Spanish, Azul honors the language that Gael and his mother share and also the use of Spanish in Gael's classroom.

Creating Learning Stories in the Context of an Inquiry Group

When you undertake the process of inquiry, documentation, and reflection alone, you are on your own as you wrestle with such questions as these: What material or data should I collect and how? What is the meaning and value of the material that I have collected? How can I use the material I collected to improve my teaching and the children's learning? Whom can I share my inquiry and document with so I can reflect more deeply?

While this solo inquiry process can be valuable, it can also be lonely, and you miss out on feedback and advice from other teacher colleague inquirers. This is where participation in an inquiry group, whether at your site or in conjunction with teachers at other sites, becomes so valuable. When educators connect Learning Stories with the professional development

Original Learning Story "One, Two, Three Steps Closer," by Azul Muller

process of participating in inquiry groups, and with the systematic collection of and reflection on material from their early childhood settings, the level of discussion and reflection becomes elevated.

Collaborative inquiry facilitates regular meetings and discussions with colleagues to review documentation and brainstorm next steps for inquiry and teaching (Escamilla & Meier 2017; Kroll & Meier 2018; Stribling 2017). It can also encourage group members to stay engaged with the inquiry process when feeling discouraged or lost with observation, documentation, and reflection. Participating in an inquiry group also allows for the exchange of questions and ideas with colleagues, families, and the wider community. And as an inquiry group grows and evolves over time,

group members learn how to trust and to share their inquiry material, take on supportive, collaborative, and leading roles, and offer each other helpful next steps for inquiry, documentation, and reflection. Further, as teacher inquirers share early drafts of documentation like photographs and artifacts that could be part of a final Learning Story, group members can provide feedback on the quality or depth of the documentation and suggest ideas for further inquiry and reflection.

In this process of "putting yourself out there," group members learn to take risks in sharing material that might reflect on their teaching and inquiry skills and knowledge. There can be feelings of nervousness and possibly even some level of fear, so the group meeting facilitator(s), structure, agenda, and protocol provide structured support for sharing and commenting. For example, over the roughly 10 years that the Las Americas inquiry group (consisting of teachers at a public preschool in San Francisco and cofacilitated by authors Isauro and Daniel) met, participants learned to trust their own feelings and each other's support through ongoing, productive conversations and perspective taking. A key element of this process was the group's communication style and method (Escamilla & Meier 2017):

> Reading out loud a Learning Story for the group to hear (emphasizing the sense of authorship of the Learning Story's creator and making the reading a communal listening experience)

> Multilingualism (such as writing a Learning Story in the first language of a child and teacher and providing multilingual translation so that other group members can understand documentation)

> Overtures for equitable turn taking (allowing and even encouraging others to take the floor: "Wesley, can you please share about those great photographs you've been taking?")

> Expansions (comments that expand and extend others' ideas and observations: "I wonder if you want to ask the children to reflect on those photographs?")

> Complementary moves (statements that indicate that others are also using a similar inquiry strategy: "This reminds me of the way that you use those sticky notes to write down what the children are wondering about")

> Language of solidarity (affirmations of collaboration and trust: "I'm still in the learning process of understanding what Learning Stories are and what they can do for us")

From Reflection to Inquiry

Reflection on your practice means that you take the time to think about what has happened in your classroom; to examine artifacts of the work that you have done and that the children have created, including your notes, photographs, audio recordings, and video recordings to jog your memory; and to help you see things that you didn't notice at the time. As you learn to do this systematically (e.g., on a regular basis, using tools you become comfortable with,

referring to your data to think ahead), you move from reflection to inquiry—to asking questions about what is happening in your classroom to teach the children and yourself better.

Inquiry can happen through various means, such as by examining artifacts (e.g., children's work or photos of children's interactions) and sharing documentation such as observation notes or even video or audio recordings of teaching and children's responses. Above all, inquiry is a stance or an attitude toward your work. It reflects a curiosity, a passion, and an interest. In taking an inquiry stance, you try not to be critical or negative about what you are doing or have done. Asking "What went right?" and "What went wrong?" are not as productive questions as "What happened here?" or "What were the children (or the teachers) thinking about here?"

Documentation: Provoking Questions and Wonderings

Documentation is key to the inquiry process and can be used to spark discussions and develop more formal inquiry questions. Documentation consists of the many materials that teacher inquirers collect over the course of a project or activity. By sharing and discussing documentation, teachers can move together from talking about general puzzling ideas or specific wonderings about an occurrence to a more focused inquiry.

Documentation can include many different kinds of artifacts, including observation notes, photographs, videos, audio recordings, children's work, group brainstorms, and Learning Stories. Participants in an inquiry group learn to experiment with a range of documentation processes and products and to see how others in the group put their own personal twist or stamp on their documentation. No documentation process or product is ever the same, nor should it be. Effective documentation comes from an organized system for collection of material as well as individual creativity and inventiveness.

Conclusion

The more you are *not* alone in your thinking, the more supported and reflective you can feel and be. There are many options for finding thinking partners, even if most of your teaching is done with just one adult and a small group of children, such as in a family child care program. Remember that there are already reflection partners in your worksite—the children and their families—and that it is also possible to reflect with folks who are not with you every day but who share common interests in thinking about this work, such as instructional coaches or resource specialists. Meeting together on a regular basis—whether weekly, biweekly, or even monthly—provides the opportunity to reflect collectively on what is occurring in your work, learn how better to reflect by yourselves, and challenge one another as critical friends to ask yourselves questions about your practice, the children, and their families.

ISAURO M. ESCAMILLA, EdD, is assistant professor in the Graduate College of Education at San Francisco State University.

LINDA R. KROLL, PhD, is professor emerita of education at the School of Education at Mills College, Oakland, California.

DANIEL R. MEIER, PhD, is professor of elementary education at San Francisco State University.

ANNIE WHITE, EdD, is associate professor in the Early Childhood Studies program at California State University Channel Islands.

CHAPTER 26

Thinking of Yourself as a Professional

Nicole Lazarte

It's a beautiful Thursday morning with the sun shining and a slight breeze in the air. Senators, House members, and advocates from across the country gather on Capitol Hill to rally around the call for urgency and widespread support for child care. They speak in unison . . . "We can do better, we will do better!"

I attended a press conference with members of Congress, families, early childhood providers, and advocacy group leaders to address key issues that impact our profession, including lowered child care costs for families and support for the child care workforce. I was honored to be invited to speak as an early childhood educator who saw and experienced the struggles on a day-to-day basis. I felt heard as I spoke alongside other passionate advocates on the Hill.

I always knew I wanted to help make a difference in the lives of children. Once I became a teacher, I did my very best to help the children and their families thrive. However, I soon realized that much more needed to be done outside of the four walls of my classroom. I turned to advocacy to speak out and share the knowledge I had of the importance of the early years. We cannot keep losing teachers due to burnout. We cannot keep losing families from programs because they cannot afford the tuition and therefore have to leave the workforce. We cannot keep losing children's chances of success because they don't have access to high-quality child care.

My colleagues and I worked for an amazing NAEYC-accredited child care center with a director who believed in and invested in us. Yet because of the overall system's challenges and underfinancing, we remained underpaid and overwhelmed, and we struggled daily to stay in jobs we loved and were good at for children and families who needed us. This job too often required us to sacrifice our own health and financial stability. This work is so much more than babysitting; child care is so much more than having a place to put children while their parents work. I am skilled, knowledgeable, and valuable; I know what quality care and education looks like and how to provide

it; and I was responsible for day-to-day interactions that influenced the developing brain architecture of children and that supported them and their families to thrive. I shouldn't have been burdened by wages that barely allowed me to make ends meet. Families shouldn't be burdened by costs that barely allow them to make ends meet either. Yet unless things change, I fear for the future of our programs, families, and children.

 EQUITY Teachers join with others to become more informed advocates and strengthen their collective impact.

Advocacy is an amazing way to be connected and be a part of something bigger. Every day, officials are creating the rules for our field without knowing the work firsthand. Who else better to speak about what works and what needs to be changed than those who do? The educators who spend their days teaching important social and emotional skills, conducting assessments, and communicating with families are the ones who can best advocate for change. We need people who are knowledgeable in child development and understand the struggles faced by educators, children, and families to speak up and share their stories. With enough voices, we can make a difference!

To begin advocating, you can reach out to your members of Congress. Let them know that significant, sustained investments in child care are needed *now*, and follow up with them. Write an op-ed about your experiences and what federal funding for child care would mean to you. Join town hall meetings. And get connected with your NAEYC Affiliate for more opportunities!

NICOLE LAZARTE was an infant lead teacher at ACCA Child Development Center in northern Virginia. She is currently the communications and advocacy specialist at NAEYC.

CHAPTER 27

Advocacy in Action
Stepping Up to Make an Impact

Maria Estlund

NAEYC's position statements on developmentally appropriate practice (2020a) and professional standards and competencies (2019b) outline expectations for early childhood educators to demonstrate professionalism. One key component is that educators identify and involve themselves with the early childhood profession and the broader system and serve as informed advocates for young children, their families, and the profession. Early childhood educators "know that equity in education begins in early childhood and that [they] have a special opportunity and responsibility to advance equity in their daily classroom work with children and their work with families and colleagues" (NAEYC 2019b, 24). Demonstrating professionalism within the context of the existing and rich diversity within the United States in general and our early childhood education system specifically means being able to successfully support, work with, see the strengths, and meet the needs of families, children, and colleagues from many different cultural, racial, linguistic, and community contexts.

This competency is especially true of infant and toddler educators, who are caring for and facilitating the development of children during their most critical first years. All educators of infants and toddlers, whether they work in child care centers, family child care homes, or children's own homes, are connected to the children's families and are in an important position to understand their needs. Educators provide support by facilitating reciprocal partnerships with families and sharing their expertise, guidance, and information on a child's development and community resources.

Infant and Toddler Educators as Advocates

The position statement on developmentally appropriate practice and the professional standards and competencies empower you to understand the broader dynamics, including public policies, that shape the early childhood system, your role as an educator, and the realities of the families you serve. You have the opportunity to advocate to make these systems better. This means engaging in advocacy within your early learning setting on behalf of children in your care, yourself, and your colleagues. You also can engage in advocacy at broader levels, such as in local, state, or national contexts. To do so requires a basic understanding of how public policies are developed and how individuals can influence decision makers.

Whether you are new to advocacy or a seasoned veteran, whether you have two minutes or two hours available, there are multiple advocacy strategies that you can engage in. Whatever your situation, you can be an advocate.

Here are some steps you might start with:

> **Learn more about early childhood policies and programs for infants and toddlers.** Early childhood educators can help the children and families they serve by understanding the supports available to them—including child care assistance, early intervention for infants and toddlers with developmental delays and disabilities, and many more—and how they can advocate for investments and improvements to these programs. NAEYC has resources on federal programs, and you can find information on state policies and programs through state Affiliates, advocacy organizations, and state agencies.

> **Participate in a community teacher or program roundtable.** Make connections with businesses and child and family resources in your community. These relationships will provide meaningful opportunities to support and impact children and families positively.

> **Connect with your state's NAEYC Affiliate organization and advocacy partner organizations.** NAEYC's network of Affiliates provides excellent opportunities for NAEYC members to participate in activities including policy- and advocacy-related activities at the state and local levels.

> **Contact your state senator and representative: email, call, post!** Your state's NAEYC Affiliate and advocacy partners share action alerts and templates so you can easily contact your legislators—be sure to sign up for newsletters and advocacy communications.

> **Contact your US senator and representative in Congress: email, call, post!** Like state partners mentioned above, NAEYC and its national advocacy partners share opportunities and tools to help you contact your federal lawmakers, including email templates and sample social media posts. Sign up for newsletters and advocacy communications from NAEYC and other national early childhood advocacy organizations to get connected to these opportunities.

> **Build relationships with your local legislators.** Reach out and introduce yourself to your state legislators, tell them you are an educator or provider in their district, and offer helpful information and resources in support of early childhood care and education. NAEYC, state Affiliates, and advocacy partners have numerous fact sheets and resources that you can share with your lawmakers.

If you're ready to make a deeper impact, try these suggestions:

> **Meet with local, state, and federal policymakers.** Share with these decision makers about the importance of early childhood, the positive impacts and innovative services that you provide, and the critical investments and policy improvements needed for the field to move forward. Be clear with your request, and make sure it is appropriate for their level of office. For example, ask your state legislators for increased state funding; ask your congressional members for increased federal investments. Connect with your state Affiliate and advocacy partners for resources and information about state-level advocacy priorities and requests. Be sure to take photos to

share on social media (and tag the policymakers!). Always follow up on your communication or conversation with policymakers.

> **Host a site visit at your program for a policymaker.** Invite local and state policymakers to come to your child care center or family child care home to see early childhood education in action and to speak with you and/or educators and colleagues. Be sure to take pictures to share on social media and tag the policymakers. Follow up with policymakers about your conversation or communication.

> **Testify at state and/or congressional legislative committee hearings, either in person or by submitting written testimony.** Committees hear testimony to support or oppose specific legislation, budget and funding requests, and general topics or issues. Connect with state and national advocacy organizations, including NAEYC, about opportunities to testify. State organizations often have testimony templates that individuals can use and personalize to show strong, aligned support in testimonies submitted.

> **Submit public comment on proposed regulations and administrative policies.** After a bill becomes a law, the implementation and regulatory details are typically fleshed out in administrative policy, rules, and regulations. Like the legislative process, this administrative policy process is public and includes opportunities for public and stakeholder input. State Affiliates and advocacy organizations track regulatory and rule-making activity and should make the field aware of proposed changes and opportunities to submit public comment sharing support, opposition, and recommendations.

Engage with the media!

> **Interview with a reporter.** Child care programs are central hubs for the community, providing access to services and resources that extend far beyond meeting a family's child care needs. Collaborate with program leaders to reach out to your local news outlet to highlight the exciting work happening in your program and the ways you are supporting families and your local community. Share some of the difficulties and challenges your program faces and how members of the community can support early childhood.

> **Write an op-ed or letter to the editor.**
> Your lived experiences and expertise make you a trusted source in your community to talk about what young children need, the type of support families with young children need, and the challenges facing the early childhood workforce and programs like yours. Utilize resources NAEYC has developed to help you get started (visit NAEYC.org/our-work/public-policy-advocacy/build-your-advocacy-skills-and-knowledge).

> **Invite press to feature your program, staff, families and/or students.** Celebrate exciting milestones in your programs and invite members of your community to celebrate with you. Consider adding members of the press to your invitation list, but before you do, make sure you are clear on what makes this celebration special and why a reporter should not want to miss participating.

Infant and toddler educators have a necessary perspective and unique opportunity to serve as an informed advocate on behalf of children, families, and the early childhood field. The position statement on developmentally appropriate practice and the professional standards and competencies expect and empower professionals to advocate for children's best interests in and out of the classroom. In turn, infant and toddler educators should expect to be valued and compensated as the professionals that they are. NAEYC advocates for policy solutions affecting infant and toddler educators that are fair and based on principles that recognize and enhance the strengths and expertise of the current and future workforce. The *Unifying Framework for the Early Childhood Education Profession* (Power to Profession Task Force 2020) provides a roadmap for elevating and supporting infant and toddler professionals—and all early childhood professionals—now and into the future (see the sidebar).

The Unifying Framework for the Early Childhood Education Profession: Opportunities for Infant and Toddler Educators

The *Unifying Framework for the Early Childhood Education Profession* was born out of the Power to the Profession (P2P; Power to the Profession Task Force 2020) initiative to define the early childhood education profession—an inclusive, multiyear process (2017–2020) that engaged more than 11,000 early childhood educators, diverse stakeholders across the early childhood field, and experts from other established professions. The outcome was the *Unifying Framework*, which puts forth several primary recommendations to establish unity and clarity around the career pathways, knowledge and competencies, qualifications, standards, accountability, supports, and compensation to define the early childhood education profession within the broader early childhood education field.

Here are key recommendations of the *Unifying Framework*:

> **A distinct profession.** Within the broader early childhood field, the "early childhood education profession" will be made up in part of those who will be called "early childhood educators," responsible for caring for and promoting the learning, development, and well-being of children birth–8.

> **One profession, three designations.** Create a structure with only three distinct and meaningful designations—Early Childhood Educator I, II, and III—and in which all early childhood educators hold a license to practice. Each designation will have an associated scope of practice, expected level of professional preparation, and expected level of mastery of the professional standards and competencies for early childhood educators.

> **Aligned professional preparation programs.** Establish a primary set of pathways, including early childhood credentials, associate degrees, and baccalaureate degrees, that will support students in meeting the competencies.

> **Professional compensation.** Increase state and federal investments in early childhood education to achieve fair compensation for the profession within a set of guiding principles.

> **Supportive infrastructure, shared accountability.** Create a broader, more coherent system, as other professions have done. In addition to early childhood educators themselves, government agencies, higher education and professional preparation programs, early childhood employers/owners, and the newly established professional governance body will all take on specific responsibilities and accountability provisions.

The *Unifying Framework* specifically calls for the need to elevate and include infant and toddler educators, noting that the standards, accountability, and levels within the early childhood education profession must be established to intentionally include and support infant and toddler educators along the way.

Implementing and achieving the vision of the *Unifying Framework* will require significant investments in funding and supportive policies at the federal and state level—and continued support and advocacy from the entire early childhood field. Teachers of infants and toddlers can play a role in advancing the *Unifying Framework* and supporting the profession.

In conclusion, consider the reflection of infant and toddler professional Xiara Quinn on the critical role advocacy has played in her career:

> The work of an infant and toddler educator is deeply interconnected with many different aspects of community systems. At some point, my investment in the well-being of children led to an investment in healthy family systems, which inevitably led to an investment in thriving communities. Suddenly, I couldn't care just about what happens within the walls of my classroom. I needed to engage with issues that impacted the lived experiences of the children in my classroom and their families. That's how advocacy became an integral part of my work as an educator and an early childhood professional.
>
> Seeking out ways to participate in advocacy and other community work from the standpoint of an infant and toddler educator has also shown me just how valuable this work is! So often early childhood educators (and especially infant and toddler educators) are placed in a box. We are told that we are only good for one thing: keeping children cared for while the parents are at work. We are treated as though we don't have much to offer beyond "being good with kids." The more I engage with my community and share my expertise, the more I learn that our communities are craving the unique perspectives of early childhood educators. Our communities need us to work beyond our boxes and use our knowledge and skills to advocate for young children.

MARIA ESTLUND, MSW, is a state policy specialist at NAEYC.

Index

insight gathered from, 47

overview, 44–45

purposes of documentation, 55

reflection on, 47–48

and scaffolding learning, 60–62

science of observation, 52–53

screenings, 46–47

sharing with families, 49–50

of STEAM learning, 109–110

steps to take following, 49–50

team strategies for, 100

value of documentation, 55

online professional resources, 117

on-site mentoring, 118

outdoor exploration, 102–104

P

parenting stages, 29–30

pause, power of, 77–78

peer interaction

facilitating inclusion of children with diverse abilities, 57, 59

and infants' learning about self and others, 64–65, 68

using emotion language during, 84, 85

perception bias, 24

physical environment. *See* environment, arranging

planning web, 65, 66, 67

play

facilitating inclusion of children with diverse abilities, 57

and infants' learning about self and others, 64–65

narrating of, 81

outdoors, 103

pointing gestures, 73–74, 75

professionalism, demonstrating

through advocacy, 125, 126–129

Learning Stories, 120–124

overview, 114–115

professional development path, 116–119

thinking of yourself as a professional, 125

R

race and racism, 20–21, 86

reading, early exploration of, 16, 88

receptive language skills, 93

reciprocal partnerships with families. *See* family engagement

redirection, using clear limits and, 68

reflection

and advocacy, 43

on assessment information, 47–48, 49

on emotions, 85, 86

and identifying bias, 22, 23, 24

and inquiry, 121–122, 123–124

and observation, 61–62

and professional growth, 119

on roles and mindsets, 30–31

and the use of silence, 78

reflective planning cycle, 65–66

relationships, as a buffer to stress, 6, 18–21

resources, professional, 96, 100, 117, 118

resources for families, 41, 43, 100

responsive relationships with multilingual children, 93–94, 95

roles

defining of, within IFSP teams, 98

reflecting on, and family interaction, 30–31

routines. *See* daily routines

S

scaffolding children's learning, 57, 60–62

screenings, 46–47

self, learning about, 63–69

self-identity exploration, 13

self-reflection. *See* reflection

sensory experiences in nature, 103

shared attention, 73–74, 103

social and emotional development

contextual considerations for, 63–69

cultivating relationships to support, 6, 18–21

using emotion language to promote, 83–86

using silence to support, 77–78

social support and professional development, 116

specialists, as team members, 96, 97

STEAM experiences, 108–113

strengths-based approach, 11–12, 14–17, 31, 35, 120

stress and trauma, 6, 8, 18–21

T

teaming strategies for inclusive settings, 96–101

Touchpoints Model of Development, 31

transition from home to program, 37–39

transition to outdoor play, 49

trauma. *See* stress and trauma

trusting relationships, 37–39

U

Unifying Framework for the Early Childhood Education Profession, 128–129

unique needs of children, 56–59, 96–101

V

vocabulary

and babbling, 73

of emotions, 84, 85

and gesturing, 74

of multilingual children, 93, 94, 95

and STEAM learning, 112, 113

teaching of, with explicit language skills, 79–82

vocalizations, 64, 72–73, 77–78

W

webinars and workshops, professional, 117

writing and emergent literacy skills, 87–88, 89

Z

zone of proximal development (ZPD), 60